LifeLight

"In Him was life, and that life was the light of men." John 1:4

Timothy, Titus, Philemon

LEADERS GUIDE

CONCORDIA PUBLISHING HOUSE • SAINT LOUIS

3558 S. Jefferson Ave., St. Louis, MO 63118-3968
1-800-325-3040 • cph.org

Earl H. Gaulke, editor

Written by Michael Henrichs and Erik J. Rottmann

Denise Muhly and Lavern Schmidt, field-test coordinators

Cover Illustration by Steven Noble

This publication may be available in Braille, in large print, or on cassette tape for the visually impaired. Please allow 8 to 12 weeks for delivery. Write to Lutheran Braille Workers, P.O. Box 5000, Yucaipa, CA 92399; call toll-free 1-800-925-6092; or visit the website: www.LBWinc.org.

Manufactured in the USA.

3 4 5 6 7 8 9 10 11 31 30 29 28 27 26 25

Contents

Introduction

Welcome to LifeLight

A special pleasure is in store for you. You will be instrumental in leading your brothers and sisters in Christ closer to Him who is our life and light (John 1:4). You will have the pleasure of seeing fellow Christians discover new insights and rediscover old ones as they open the Scriptures and dig deep into them, perhaps deeper than they have ever dug before. More than that, you will have the pleasure of sharing in this wonderful study.

LifeLight—An In-depth Study

LifeLight is a series of in-depth Bible studies. The goal of LifeLight is that through a regular program of in-depth personal and group study of Scripture, more and more Christian adults may grow in their personal faith in Jesus Christ, enjoy fellowship with the members of His body, and reach out in love to others in witness and service.

In-depth means that this Bible study includes the following four components: individual daily home study; discussion in a small group; a lecture presentation on the Scripture portion under study; and an enhancement of the week's material (through reading the enrichment magazine).

LifeLight Participants

LifeLight participants are adults who desire a deeper study of the Scriptures than is available in the typical Sunday morning adult Bible class. (Mid-to-older teens might also be LifeLight participants.) While LifeLight does not assume an existing knowledge of the Bible or special experience or skills in Bible study, it does assume a level of commitment that will bring participants to each of the nine weekly assemblies having read the assigned readings and attempted to answer the study questions. Daily reading and study will require from 15 to 30 minutes for the five days preceding the LifeLight assembly. The day following the assembly will be spent reviewing the previous week's study by going over the completed study leaflet and the enrichment magazine.

LifeLight Leadership

While the in-depth process used by LifeLight begins with individual study and cannot achieve its aims without this individual effort, it cannot be completed by individual study alone. Therefore, trained leaders are necessary. You fill one or perhaps more of the important roles described below.

The Director

This person oversees the LifeLight program in a local center (which may be a congregation or a center operated by several neighboring congregations). The director

- serves as the parish LifeLight overall coordinator and leader;
- coordinates the scheduling of the LifeLight program;
- orders materials;
- convenes LifeLight leadership team meetings;
- develops publicity materials;
- recruits participants;
- maintains records and budgeting;
- assigns, with the leadership team, participants to small discussion groups;
- makes arrangements for facilities;
- communicates outreach opportunities to small-group leaders and to congregational boards;
- follows up on participants who leave the program.

The Assistant Director *(optional)*

This person may assist the director. Duties listed for the director may be assigned to the assistant director as mutually agreeable.

The Lecture Leader

This person prepares and delivers the lecture at the weekly assembly. **(Lesson material for the lecture leader begins on p. 9.)** The lecture leader

- prepares and presents the Bible study lecture to the large group;
- prepares worship activities (devotional thought, hymn, prayer), using resources in the study leaflet and leaders guide and possibly other, outside sources;
- helps the small-group discussion leaders to grow in understanding the content of the lessons;
- encourages prayer at weekly leadership-team and discussion-leaders meetings.

The Small-Group Coordinator *(optional; the director may fill this role)*

This person supervises and coordinates the work of the small-group discussion leaders. The small-group coordinator

- recruits with the leadership team the small-group discussion leaders;
- trains or arranges for training of the discussion leaders;
- assists the director and discussion leaders in follow-up and outreach;
- encourages the discussion leaders to contact absent group members;
- participates in the weekly leadership-team and discussion-leaders equipping meetings;
- provides ongoing training and support as needed.

The Small-Group Discussion Leaders

These people guide and facilitate discussion of LifeLight participants in the small groups. **(Lesson material for the small-group leaders begins on p. 46.)** There should be one discussion leader for every group of no more than 12 participants. The small-group discussion leaders are, perhaps, those individuals who are most important to the success of the program. They should, therefore, be chosen with special care and be equipped with skills needed to guide discussion and to foster a caring fellowship within the group. These discussion leaders

- prepare each week for the small-group discussion by using the study leaflet and small-group leaders guide section for that session **(see p. 46)**;
- read the enrichment magazine as a study supplement;
- guide and facilitate discussion in their small group;
- encourage and assist the discussion group in prayer;
- foster fellowship and mutual care within the discussion group;
- attend weekly discussion-leaders training meetings.

Leadership Training

LifeLight leaders will meet weekly to review the previous week's work and plan the coming week. At this session, leaders can address concerns and prepare for the coming session. LifeLight is a 1½-hour program with no possibility for it to be taught in the one hour typically available on Sunday mornings. Some congregations, however, may want to use the Sunday morning Bible study hour for LifeLight preparation and leadership training. In such a meeting, the lecture leader and/or small-group coordinator may lead the discussion leaders through the coming week's lesson, reserving 5 or 10 minutes for problem solving or other group concerns.

While it requires intense effort, LifeLight has proven to be of great benefit to LifeLight participants. The effort put into this program, both by leaders and by participants, will be rewarding and profitable.

The LifeLight Weekly Schedule

Here is how LifeLight will work week by week:

1. Before session 1, each participant will receive the study leaflet for session 1 and the enrichment magazine for the course. The study leaflet contains worship resources (for use both in individual daily study and at the opening of the following week's assembly) and readings and study questions for five days. Challenge questions will lead those participants who have the time and desire a greater challenge into even deeper levels of study.
2. After the five days of individual study at home, participants will gather for a weekly assembly of all LifeLight participants. The assembly will begin with a brief period of worship (5 minutes). Participants will then join their assigned small discussion groups (of 12 or fewer, who will remain the same throughout the course), where they will go over the week's study questions together (55 minutes). Assembling together once again, participants will listen to a lecture presentation on the readings they have studied in the previous week and discussed in their small groups (20 minutes). After the lecture presentation, the director or another leader will distribute the study leaf-

let for the following week. Closing announcements and other necessary business may take another five minutes before dismissal.

In some places some small groups will not join the weekly assembly because of scheduling or other reasons. Such groups may meet at another time and place (perhaps in the home of one of the small group's members). They will follow the same schedule, but they may use a cassette tape to listen to the week's lecture presentation. The discussion leader will obtain the tape and leaflets from the director. A congregation may record the lecture given by the lecture leader at the weekly assembly and duplicate it for use by other groups meeting later in the week.

3. On the day following the assembly, participants will review the preceding week's work by rereading the study leaflet they completed (and that they perhaps supplemented or corrected during the discussion in their small group) and by reading appropriate articles in the enrichment magazine.

Then the LifeLight weekly study process will begin all over again!

Recommended Study and Worship Resources

Concordia Self-Study Bible, New International Version. St. Louis: Concordia Publishing House, 1986. Interpretive notes on each page form a running commentary on the text. The book includes cross-references, a 35,000-word concordance, full-color maps, charts, and time lines.

The Holy Bible, English Standard Version: Concordia Edition. St. Louis: Concordia Publishing House for Crossway Bibles, 2001, 2003. An accurate and precise word-for-word translation where each word and phrase is carefully weighed against the original Hebrew, Aramaic, and Greek to ensure the fullest accuracy and clarity.

Lenski, R.C.H. *The Interpretation of St. Paul's Epistles to the Colossians, to the Thessalonians, to Timothy, to Titus, and to Philemon.* Minneapolis: Augsburg Publishing House, 1961. This volume (originally published by Lutheran Book Concern, Columbus, Ohio, 1937) is a reliable commentary by a Lutheran theologian.

Roehrs, Walter R., and Martin H. Franzmann. *Concordia Self-Study Commentary.* St. Louis: Concordia Publishing House, 1979. This one-volume commentary on the Bible contains 950 pages and is tailored for lay use.

Schuetze, Armin W. *1 Timothy, 2 Timothy, Titus.* In the People's Bible Commentary Series. St. Louis: Concordia Publishing House, 1993. Weaves the New International Version (NIV) of the texts with an in-depth commentary to enrich understanding.

Every Voice a Song: Pipe Organ Accompaniment for 180 Hymns and Liturgical Songs. St. Louis: Concordia Publishing House (order no. 99-1565). Use this music CD for worship hymn accompaniment.

To a True Son in the Faith

1 Timothy 1

Preparing for the Session

Central Focus

Paul begins his Letter to Timothy by focusing on the vital importance of sound doctrine (that is, teaching) for the Christian church. The Gospel is essential to the church's life, for it gives the divine gift of faith even to blasphemers and persecutors and violent men (1 Timothy 1:13). Yet the Law is also good, and it must be used properly (1 Timothy 1:8). The church's faithful teaching of the pure Word of God—both Law and Gospel—must never become mixed with false teachings, because such falsehoods will only lead people away from the faith.

Objectives

That the participant, as a child of God and with the Holy Spirit's help, will be led deeper into the divinely given realizations that

1. in its earliest days, the church already struggled with false teachers;
2. both God's Law and His Gospel remain essential to the individual Christian's faith and life;
3. when God's Word is no longer taken seriously in the church, but gets replaced by "vain discussion" (1 Timothy 1:6), Christians will inevitably make "shipwreck of their faith" (1 Timothy 1:19).

Note for the small-group leaders: Lesson notes and other materials you will need begin on page 46.

For the Lecture Leader

Session Plan

Worship

Begin the session with the hymn printed in the study leaflet. Accompaniments are available in denominational hymnals, such as *Lutheran Worship* (*LW*, refer to hymnal index). (Note: Concordia Publishing House has available *Every Voice a Song*, a 9-CD set of organ accompaniments for 180 hymns and liturgy. All the initial worship hymns in the LifeLight courses are included in this resource. It's especially helpful for mission congregations and small parishes. See the list of study resources on page 7.) Follow with this prayer:

Prayer

Blessed Lord, since You have caused all Holy Scriptures to be written for our learning, grant that we may so hear them, read, mark, learn and take them to heart that by patience and comfort of Your holy Word we may embrace and ever hold fast the blessed hope of everlasting life, through Jesus Christ, our Lord. Amen (*LW*, p. 156).

Lecture Presentation

This is the first of two Letters that Paul wrote to Timothy, a young pastor in Ephesus. Timothy appears to have his hands full with false teachers, and Paul begins by reminding Timothy that one of his duties in Ephesus is to oppose such creators of division and controversy. Yet Timothy is not defenseless; he has the powerful Word of God. This Word created faith in even "the worst of sinners" (1 Timothy 1:16 NIV)! Certainly it will guard and protect God's chosen pastor and his congregation against those who wish to destroy the faith by their false teaching!

1 Opening Greeting (1:1–2)

Verse 1—Because ancient letters were customarily written on scrolls, the writer's name often appeared at the beginning, along with a self-description. That way, the reader could see who wrote the letter without unrolling it entirely. Paul's self-description is important, even though Timothy already knew him well. Here Paul indicates the authority by which he speaks: he is an apostle (that is, a "sent one") by the command of the Father and the Son. This self-description is somewhat like church letterhead with the pastor's name in the heading.

By describing himself as an apostle, as he habitually does, Paul sets himself apart from the "certain persons" (1 Timothy 1:3) who have no call and no apostleship. Paul speaks because God commands him to speak; these others insinuate themselves into the congregation.

Verse 2—The Letter is addressed to Pastor Timothy, but it might also have been read aloud during worship. Paul describes Timothy as a son (Philippians 2:22), as he did Titus (Titus 1:4) and the slave Onesimus (Philemon 10). This description suggests Paul's great, fatherly love for his fellow workers, including Timothy whom he greets here with "grace, mercy and peace from God."

2 Oppose Those Who Teach Falsely! (1:3–7)

Verses 3–4—Paul's trip to Macedonia is not mentioned in Acts, which suggests that it took place after his three main missionary journeys. Paul urges Timothy to remain in Ephesus for the expressed purpose of opposing false teachers. The work might not be as glamorous as traveling the world, but it is necessary for the life and health of the church. Though young (1 Timothy 4:12), Timothy had received sufficient theological training and experience at Paul's own hand. He may now be entrusted with the pastoral task. Given pastoral authority to guard the Ephesian flock, Timothy must "charge" or give strict orders about what sort of teaching the congregation will be allowed to hear.

It is unclear what exactly Paul means by "myths and endless genealogies." What is clear is that these had begun to compete with the Word of God for authority in the church. Trouble results when such things are considered more important than the Scriptures. This happens even in today's church life whenever personal opinions, group decisions, church constitutions, and so forth attempt to compete for authority over God's Word.

Verse 5—Paul does not tell Timothy to be authoritative and to give commands because he wants Timothy to lord his position over the congregation. Rather, "the aim of our charge is love." Timothy will oppose the false teachers because he loves the church and her members. Some of the people in his congregation will not like the things Timothy must say and do. But Timothy is a caring pastor, not a warlord. His conscience forces him to oppose false teaching and his divinely-given faith stirs him to action. Timothy's heart—cleansed by the Gospel of Christ—beats with love and devotion toward the very people he preaches against, as well as those whom they attempt to mislead.

Verses 6–7—The false teachers must be stopped because their falsehoods put Christian faith and salvation into jeopardy. Paul's words include a hint of ridicule: they don't even know what they are talking about! Some of today's so-called Bible experts sound equally ridiculous when they claim that God does not oppose homosexuality and abortion, say there is no resurrection, or believe that the Bible is not truly the inspired, inerrant, powerful Word of God.

3 The Law Is Good (1:8–11)

Verse 8—It might seem that Paul abruptly changes topics, first talking about the false teachers and then about the Law. Yet things will fit into place if we assume that the false teachers might have been teaching against God's Law, claiming that it no longer has value for the church.

Even today, some people in the church say that the Law of God is no longer applicable and that we live by the Gospel alone. But Paul insists that the Law is good, so long as it is used properly. The Law does not give salvation. Salvation is given when the Holy Spirit connects you to Christ's death and resurrection. Yet the Law is good because the Spirit uses it to do the good work of revealing your sin and creating sorrow over it. This makes you ready to hear the Good News of the Gospel, the Good News that God now forgives your every sin for the sake of Christ.

Verses 9–11—If everyone were righteous and holy, the Law would serve no purpose, because it does not attack righteousness. It attacks sin. Therefore, the Law is for sinners. And look at all the ways sin manifests itself! Yet when we honestly examine our own hearts in light of the Ten Commandments, who among us could ever claim that we are not sinful in every way? This is part of the good and proper work that the Law does—it shows us our sin.

The Law also attacks false teaching and "whatever else is contrary to sound doctrine [teaching], in accordance with the glorious gospel." False teachers not only sin against the Ten Commandments—showing lovelessness both for God and neighbor—but they also rob the church of the Gospel. For this reason, Paul, Timothy, and pastors and Christians of all time must concern themselves with the Word of God's Law and His Gospel, insisting that both always be taught in truth, purity, and fullness.

4 The Gospel Works Miracles in Lawbreakers (1:12–17)

Verses 12–13—Paul now offers himself as an example of what happens to sinners when they are crushed by God's Law and given faith through His Gospel. Don't be fooled by the wording here: it is not that Christ "judged" Paul faithful in the sense that He looked at Paul and said, "Wow! He is really faithful!" Rather, Christ *reckoned* Paul faithful or *counted* him as faithful. Compare this with Romans 4:3, which states that God "credited" (NIV) Abraham as righteous. In the same way, Christ Jesus credited Paul with faithfulness and appointed him to service, even though Paul was formerly a blasphemer and a persecutor. Ever the Faithful One, the Lord also strengthens Paul for his task.

Verse 14—As a persecutor of the church, Paul ignorantly believed that he was acting faithfully. However, the Gospel Ananias proclaimed to him in Acts 9 changed all of that. "The grace of our Lord overflowed for" him, giving him the forgiveness, salvation, faith, and love that come only from Christ Jesus.

Verse 15—Paul is not unique either. Christ Jesus did not come into this world to save only him, but all sinners. The all-encompassing forgiveness that Christ earned with His death and resurrection is often called the Universal Atonement. That is, Christ shed His blood for ALL people of every time and place. There is no one for whom Christ did not die. As we will hear later in this Letter, God also wants everyone to be connected to this salvation (1 Timothy 2:4).

When Paul calls himself the worst of sinners, he is not literally suggesting that he has sinned more than all men. He is speaking about his perception of himself, created by the Holy Spirit through the Ten Commandments. He sees that he sins against every element of God's Law; he knows that he in no way deserves God's grace. Yet God is merciful even to Paul. All Christians ought to look at themselves in the same way: saved not by any personal merit or worthiness, but purely by God's grace shown to them in Christ.

Verse 16—Notice how Paul humbly explains the reason for his salvation! He does not say that he was saved because he was going to do great things for God. Rather, Paul was saved so "Jesus Christ might display His perfect patience." It is as if Paul says, "If Jesus is powerful enough to save *me* from sin and death, He can save anybody! If He was patient with the one who so aggressively blasphemed and persecuted His church, He will be patient with all! I am a good example of God's miraculous work, for He has raised me up from the dead to eternal life, given me the gift of faith by which I believe and am saved."

Verse 17—Praise and honor for the Gospel belongs only to God. Yet when the false teachers throw away the Law, they throw away the Gospel as well. This robs God of His honor and strips Him of His glory.

5 Remain Firm in the Faith (1:18–20)

Verses 18–19a—Before the New Testament was completed, God spoke to His people through prophetic utterances in addition to preaching from the Scriptures. Paul could be speaking about a prophetic utterance that was made concerning Timothy, or he might be referring to the sermon preached at Timothy's ordination. How can we know for sure? Either way, God clearly set Timothy apart to "fight the good fight" (NIV) in his pastoral work in Ephesus. The context of this Letter suggests that Timothy's fight includes both his own perseverance in the faith (similar to 2 Timothy 4:7) and his careful protection of God's people.

What does Timothy's good fight entail? Two things: Keeping the Christian faith whole and unadulterated, and keeping the good conscience that arises from the forgiveness of sins. A good conscience itself is a gift from God. It listens to the Word of God and desires to act accordingly. Like a sheep, the conscience follows the voice of the Good Shepherd in His Word and preaching. Pastor Timothy should prefer to face rejection by the false teachers and others rather than suffer a bad conscience.

Verses 19b–20—The false teachers have rejected both faith and conscience. They teach in a way that is contrary to the clear Word of God, and they also teach contrary to their own hearts, upon which the Law of God is written (Romans 2:15). Their own words will condemn them, for they have led themselves into a shipwrecked faith.

Paul has already dealt with two men in particular. The reference to handing them over to Satan refers to church discipline, which is carried out in order to protect the congregation from similar sin and to call those who were disciplined back to repentance and faith. By denouncing their sin and separating them from the church (excommunication), Paul hopes that Hymenaeus and Alexander will realize the error of their "shipwreck" and call out to God again for His grace and mercy. Such gifts God is only too happy to provide!

Conclusion

"At the end of chapter 1 we hear how Paul gives Timothy this command, that he wage good warfare by keeping a good conscience. He gave an example about those who rejected faith and a good conscience and suffered shipwreck. These he consigned to Satan. This example he wrote to strengthen us and to terrify the [false teachers], because it is a rule that whoever has started to neglect faith and conscience soon becomes a heretic . . . . Paul therefore finds that all heretics rise from this source, that they begin to weary of this general doctrine of faith, love, and the cross. Because they are unaffected by this doctrine, they find new doctrines every day. . . . The man who begins to hold a worthless conscience and faith is not in a little danger but in the greatest and most terrible peril, because he is not merely breaking a leg in this shipwreck but is drowned completely" (Luther's Works, vol. 28, pp. 253–54).

Paul admonishes Timothy to "charge certain persons not to teach any different doctrine" (v. 3) and "wage the good warfare, holding faith and a good conscience" (vv. 18–19). He does not command legalism, but he calls Timothy to sincere love for the congregation entrusted to his care, in order that they may never wander away from the green pastures of Christ's forgiveness and into a wasteland of unbelief. Careful teaching and sound doctrine do not oppose Christian love; they are the very expressions of the Christian love that God creates for us in Christ Jesus and enables us to show to our neighbor. This love and this doctrine must remain constant, whether or not our neighbor will respond to it. Love indeed covers many sins and wrongs, but sound doctrine (teaching) must not be attacked, overlooked, treated lightly, or taken for granted.

Concluding Activities

Distribute the enrichment magazine and encourage participants to read it as part of their weekly study. Then distribute the study leaflet for the next session. Pray the following prayer:

O God, whose infinite love restores to the right way all those who err, gathers the scattered, and preserves those whom You have gathered, of Your tender mercy pour out on Your Christian people the grace of unity that, all schisms being healed, Your flock, gathered to the true Shepherd of Your church, may serve You in all faithfulness; through Jesus Christ, our Lord. Amen (*LW*, p. 126).

Join together in praying the Lord's Prayer, and then depart with the salutation:

L: The Lord be with you!

C: And also with you!

Living the Faith Together

1 Timothy 2–3

Preparing for the Session

Central Focus

1 Timothy 3:14 summarizes this section: "I am writing these things to you so that, if I delay, you may know how one ought to behave in the household of God." First Paul warns Timothy about those who use the truth for their own gain (session 1). Then he outlines the way God's household must order and conduct itself in its response to the Word of truth. The things Paul mentions here—intercessory prayer, the conduct of women, the characteristics of a pastor—flow from the life-giving Word of God. Paul recognizes that these things might not be self-evident to the church and that they might not measure up to human logic because "the mystery of godliness is great" (1 Timothy 3:16 NIV).

Objectives

That the participant, as a child of God and with the Holy Spirit's help, will be led deeper into the divinely given realizations that

1. the church, the body of Christ, has a certain shape and order according to the Gospel of salvation;
2. the individual Christian's place in the church has to do with divinely created love for God and love for neighbor, not personal gain;
3. "the mystery of godliness" (1 Timothy 3:16) requires that each Christian listen to God's truth and hold it, not pass judgment on it or decide whether it personally applies.

Note for the small-group leaders: Lesson notes and other materials you will need begin on page 49.

For the Lecture Leader

Session Plan

Worship

Begin the session with the Invocation and the hymn printed in the study leaflet. Accompaniments are available in denominational hymnals, such as *Lutheran Worship* (refer to hymnal index). (Note: Concordia Publishing House has available *Every Voice a Song,* a 9-CD set of organ accompaniments for 180 hymns and liturgy. All the initial worship hymns in the LifeLight courses are included in this resource. It's especially helpful for mission congregations and small parishes. See the list of study resources on page 7.)

Prayer

Blessed Lord, since You have caused all Holy Scriptures to be written for our learning, grant that we may so hear them, read, mark, learn and take them to heart that by patience and comfort of Your holy Word we may embrace and ever hold fast the blessed hope of everlasting life, through Jesus Christ, our Lord. Amen (*LW*, p. 156).

Lecture Presentation

1 Intercessory Prayer (2:1–8)

Verses 1–2—The words "first of all" stress the importance of the church's intercessory prayers for all people. Not only do Christians present their requests to God, but they pray with thanksgiving, knowing by faith that all things are in the heavenly Father's good care. Paul singles out "kings and all who are in high positions." This might have come as a surprise to Christians living under pagan kings like Nero, who was in power at the time. But then Paul gives his reason: "that we may lead a peaceful and quiet life, godly and dignified in every way." A good government provides quiet living to Christians and to all people because it curbs evil, allowing us to conduct our business and care for our families in relative peace—much greater peace than anarchy would allow. For this reason, the prayers of the church often remember the nations, our government, and those serving in the military. Such petitions are good prayers during both wartime and peacetime, prayed by congregations in worship and by individuals in their daily devotions.

Verses 3–4—Prayers that please God are those prayed through faith and trust in Jesus. Such prayers also show the church's concern for the salvation of the entire world, which God Himself desires. There is no one for whom Christ did not shed His blood and die, and there is no one whom God wishes to damn. People face His judgment because of their rejection of the ransom Christ earned for all—so we need to be witnessing to all!

Verses 5–6—In offering its requests and intercessions, the church essentially lives the life of Christ in the world. Jesus Himself continually pleads our case before the Father, pointing to the punishment He bore for us on the cross. In the same way, we also plead the case of others before Him, asking God to deal mercifully with them, give them the gift of faith, and include them among His people.

Notice how Paul emphasizes the human nature of Christ in this passage: "the man Christ Jesus" (1 Timothy 2:5). This counters some of the false claims, already becoming popular in some parts of the church, which suggested that Jesus is only God who took the shape of a man, but did not truly become man. Ever careful to teach "sound doctrine" (1 Timothy 1:10), Paul faithfully opposes and corrects every falsehood that creeps into the church.

Verse 7—Paul's own place in the church flows out of the life and faith that Christ Jesus created for him by becoming "a ransom for all" (1 Timothy 2:6). Paul assures the reader that he is speaking the truth, because it may sound strange that a former Pharisee and devoted enemy of the Gospel would become a herald (or "preacher"), an apostle ("one who is sent"), and a teacher of faith to the Gentiles.

Verse 8—In verse 4, where Paul states that God desires to save all men, the word used for "man" is *anthropos*, which means "human" or "person." God wants all people to be saved, males and females. Here in verse 8, Paul uses the word *andros*, referring specifically to males. Men are to provide leadership for joint worship by a group of Christians that may include both males and females (1 Corinthians 11:5), and other texts indicate that women also prayed in the public worship services.

The phrase "lifting holy hands" does not necessarily prescribe a certain bodily position, but it speaks of the holiness created for us by our Lord Jesus Christ. Because of His rich, ongoing forgiveness, God looks at us as sinless and innocent, unstained by the shedding of innocent blood, by theft or rebellion. The pastor who leads God's people in worship does not hold this position by divine right, but by the same forgiving grace and mercy that extends to all people, lifting up holy hands that have been purified by the blood of Christ.

2 The Conduct of Christian Women (2:9–15)

Verses 9–10—In a world and society in which fashion has become increasingly sensual, Paul's words here come as a timely corrective. The way people dress speaks about the way they view themselves and the world around them. Rather than dressing in a way that makes the individual's body the focus of the world's attention, Christians dress "with modesty and self-control." Their life in the church is not about their getting noticed, but it is about their gathering together with all God's saints around God's gifts of Word, Baptism, and Holy Communion. The things that get noticed are not the gold and the pearls with which the saints adorn themselves, but the good deeds that Jesus Himself commends to us: "In the same way, let your light shine before others, so that they may see your good works and give glory to your Father who is in heaven." (Matthew 5:16).

Verses 11–12—Contrary to what many people claim today, Paul does not consider women to be second-class citizens by barring them from the pastoral ministry. Everyone has their own, God-given place in the body of Christ. Many men do not qualify for the pastoral office either! Yet because Americans are so used to thinking in terms of civil rights (an idea found in the U.S. Constitution but not in the Holy Bible), sometimes people struggle with what Paul is saying here. In the church, women must not exert authority over men. Would that all men took their divinely-given responsibility seriously, both in the church and in the home! If they did, the issue of women's leadership in the church would not be nearly so critical as it now is.

Verses 13–14—The authority of a man is not Paul's own idea, but it is the basic order of the Creator's world, as his reference to Genesis suggests. Adam failed to exercise authority over Eve by not faithfully teaching her and requiring her to follow the Word. When Eve rejected Adam's authority, she "was deceived and became a transgressor." The perfect balance that God had created suddenly fell apart when man and woman abandoned the place that God had given to each. In the church, the reestablishment of the original creation has begun, brought about by the sacrifice of Christ. For this reason, the people of God pattern themselves after the created order and not after the priorities and convictions of the fallen world.

Verse 15—Paul does not intend that men are saved by faith but women are saved by having babies! Christian women are delivered *through the midst of childbirth* by the graciousness of God. Recall the curse that resulted when Eve rejected Adam's authority (Genesis 3:16). Even though the burden and penalty for Eve's sin remains for all women, they are yet saved by the grace of God despite this suffering. As they struggle in their painful deliveries of children, they need not think that God has abandoned them or that they must shed their blood in this way to atone for sin. Christ has done that for them through the shedding of His blood for their sake. Salvation remains for all who "continue in faith and love and holiness, with self-control," even amidst the rigors of childbirth.

3 The Conduct and Characteristics of the Pastor (3:1–13)

Verse 1—The word used here for "overseer" is the same word from which we get the English word *Episcopal*. Sometimes translated as "bishop," it refers to the Office of the Holy Ministry. The man who would aspire to seek (literally, "stretch oneself out toward") this office certainly does desire a noble task. The task ought not to be taken lightly or without careful consideration. Not everyone who wants the "noble task" will be called upon to fulfill it, just as not everyone who wants to be the president of the United States will get elected. Here Paul provides Timothy with a way of examining the men in his congregation, in order to distinguish those who are qualified from those who simply desire the work. Noble desire is only the first step!

Verses 2–5—The characteristics described here could rightly be applied to all Christians. However, these things most especially apply to the one who takes the pastoral office, because he represents (1) Christ to the congregation and (2) the congregation to the community and world. The ambassador of the Lord reflects in his speech, his family life, and in his daily conduct those things that fit the proclamation of the Gospel. Temperate and balanced in all things, the pastor continually battles against the impulses of the flesh (as do, of course, all Christians). The faithful management of his family is not a secondary thought, but it is as essential as all the other characteristics, for "if someone does not know how to manage his own household, how will he care for God's church?" Surely the pastor and his family experience the same temptations, struggles, and conflicts that are laid upon all Christian families. And surely we would never say that the pastor must never fail or need forgiveness. But he is an example to other pastors and to the Christians he is given to lead. He must remain their example in pious living and in wholehearted contrition and faith in Jesus alone for his salvation.

Verse 6—Paul warns that the candidate for the pastoral office must not be a recent convert, lest he become conceited in his work. A man uneducated in the Scriptures and inexperienced in the church will likely view his position in the way that earthly kings view their position, thinking that he is to be served rather than to serve.

Verse 7—The man who holds the pastoral office and preaches faithfully will undoubtedly give the world plenty of reason to despise and hate him. He need not add to their hatred by slovenly living. His life "above reproach" (v. 2) must also include "a good reputation with outsiders" (NIV). This way, his preaching will not be discredited by his lifestyle and lead to disgrace not only for himself, but also for the body of Christ, the church.

Verses 8–12—After describing the "overseer" or pastor (vv. 1–7), Paul now turns to those who would serve the church as deacons. The deaconate was an early church office that was devoted to assisting the pastoral office in attending to the day-to-day needs of the church. Deacons were not pastors but were pastoral assistants who enabled the pastor to focus his attention on "prayer and to the ministry of the word" (Acts 6:4). The characteristics here described are parallel to those required of the overseer. Many congregations and church bodies today are reexamining the role of the deaconate in the life of the church, especially with regard to parishes no longer able to support a full-time pastor. This passage from 1 Timothy suggests that special care ought to be taken in these deliberations, that a deaconate not be established as a *replacement for* the pastoral office, but that it serve in *assistance to* the pastoral office.

Verse 13—The Scriptures have clearly established that no one—man, woman, pastor, or layperson—earns salvation. This gift comes solely by the grace of God and is earned for us entirely by the suffering and death of our Lord Jesus Christ. We make no contribution at all.

Yet Paul here indicates that those who have served well gain great assurance in their faith. Because the Holy Spirit enables faith and creates love in your heart, you may look at your acts of love as expressions of God's work in you. You have not done these things, but God has done them through you! As such, you may then look upon these good fruits as assurances—in addition to the promises you regularly receive in His Word and His gifts—that you truly have God's gift of salvation and eternal life.

4 The Mystery of Godliness (3:14–16)

Verses 14–15—Paul's plans regularly change. He intends to visit Timothy in Ephesus, but he knows that his best plans may not work out. So he has sent this Letter as a way of continuing his preaching, even when he is absent.

Verse 16—By speaking of "the mystery of godliness," Paul is not suggesting that the Christian faith is a secret organization in possession of secret knowledge that no one else can have. A "mystery" in the Scriptures is something that is unknowable, except by God's revelation. The knowledge of truly pious living and godliness does not simply spring up in the Christian heart and mind, but it comes through hearing God's Word. Faith produces fruit, and faith itself is produced by the Gospel. For this reason, Paul ends this section by the proclamation of our Lord's labors for us and for our salvation, quoting an ancient hymn that might even have already been familiar to the saints in Ephesus.

Conclusion

The Gospel of our Lord Jesus Christ forms the bookends for this section (2:3–6; 3:16). From this Gospel flows all things in the church, and everything receives its shape and form from it. Paul has not yet addressed every facet of congregational life that arises from the Gospel, but he has made a beginning here and will continue through the rest of this First Letter to Timothy.

Closing Activities

Mention again the Enrichment Magazine and encourage participants to read it as part of their weekly study. Then distribute the study leaflet for the next session. Pray the following prayer:

Merciful God, we humbly implore You to cast the bright beams of Your light upon Your church that we, being instructed by the doctrine of the blessed apostles, may walk in the light of Your truth and at length attain to the light of everlasting life; through Jesus Christ, our Lord. Amen (*LW*, p. 124).

Join together in praying the Lord's Prayer, and then depart with the salutation:

L: The Lord be with you!

C: And also with you!

The Truths of the Faith Must Remain Central

1 Timothy 4:1–6:2

Preparing for the Session

Central Focus

A "good servant of Christ Jesus" (4:6) must rebuke those who teach and believe falsely. He must also care for the congregation, especially widows and older men. He must allow no one to abuse (1) the congregation (as might the young widows who want to be placed on the shut-in list without cause), or (2) the good graces of the Christian brother (such as the slave who has a believing master might be tempted). In so doing, the pastor must neither lord his position over the congregation nor allow anyone to look down on him because of the lowliness of his person. His exemplary life will help create the respect that the divinely given pastoral office deserves.

Objectives

That the participant, as a child of God and with the Holy Spirit's help, will be led deeper into the divinely given realizations that

1. the "truths of the faith," drawn from the Scriptures, must remain central in the life of every congregation;
2. the individual Christian's place in the church has to do with the humility that flows from divinely created love for God and love for neighbor, not personal gain (as we also saw in session 2);
3. pastor and congregation alike must view the pastoral office with love and respect, given by God for the care of God's people, not for the exaltation of one person or group over another.

Note for the small-group leaders: Lesson notes and other materials you will need begin on page 52.

For the Lecture Leader

Session Plan

Worship

Begin the session with the hymn printed in the study leaflet. Accompaniments are available in denominational hymnals, such as *Lutheran Worship* (refer to hymnal index). (Note: Concordia Publishing House has available *Every Voice a Song,* a 9-CD set of organ accompaniments for 180 hymns and liturgy. All the initial worship hymns in the LifeLight courses are included in this resource. It's especially helpful for mission congregations and small parishes. See the list of study resources on page 7.)

Prayer

Blessed Lord, since You have caused all Holy Scriptures to be written for our learning, grant that we may so hear them, read, mark, learn and take them to heart that by patience and comfort of Your holy Word we may embrace and ever hold fast the blessed hope of everlasting life, through Jesus Christ, Your Son, our Lord. Amen (*LW,* p. 156).

Lecture Presentation

Introduction

Paul begins this section by warning that false teachers will always be a nuisance to the church and to those pastors who preach and teach pure doctrine. Such teachers devote "themselves to deceitful spirits and teachings of demons" (4:1) and entice others to follow and do the same. Against these, Timothy must preach and teach the Scriptures faithfully. He must call upon Christians of every station in life to live according to the pure Word of God and not allow themselves to contradict the Word in speech or action. This section of 1 Timothy will move every Christian to pray, "Help us to do this, dear Father in heaven!"

1 The Challenge Timothy Faces (4:1–5)

Verses 1–2—Paul is not talking only about the future when he says "in later times." He speaks about a problem that has already arisen in the church, as indicated by the present-tense verbs in the subsequent verses. (For example, he says "who forbid" rather than "who will forbid.") Their teachings are not from God, as good as they might sound. They follow "deceitful spirits and teachings of demons." Because they have "seared" their own consciences, they have desensitized themselves to the truth. They are liars who no longer recognize their own lies, and they persist in leading others down the same damning path.

Verse 3—These false teachers had thrown away God's Word, replacing it with what seemed right in their own eyes. In particular, their falsehoods had to do with forbidding marriage and with dietary laws. Similarly, marriage is rejected in the church today not only by those who forbid it to clergy, but also by those who advocate or tolerate premarital cohabitation, homosexuality, and divorce without scriptural cause.

Verses 4–5—Paul's false teachers advocated a withdrawal from the good gifts of creation, particularly marriage and food. But Paul declares that "everything created by God is good . . . if it is received with thanksgiving." When a person enters into marriage for his own selfish purposes and leaves it again for the same reason, marriage is not good. But when marriage is cherished as God's gift of love to you, by which you may love your neighbor, it is a wonderful gift from above! Likewise, food consumed through love of self (gluttony) is not good. However, when food is viewed as God's gracious gift (as we view it with every table prayer), it must not be despised as evil.

2 Timothy Is Able to Face the Challenge of the False Teachers (4:6–16)

Verse 6—Timothy and all faithful pastors must "put these things before the brothers." Such preaching is part of what makes "a good servant." The standard by which we judge a pastor good or bad is not our own opinion of the man. Rather, we judge him good by his faithfulness to God's Word and by his willingness to warn the church of the dangers of false teaching.

Verses 7–8—Paul throws another dart at the false teachers, calling their preaching "irreverent, silly myths." Timothy must have nothing to do with such things. Training for true godliness will not involve the strict living of monkish celibacy or dietary laws, which look only to the future without joy for today. True godliness comes from holding the promise of the Gospel, not from certain actions or behaviors. True godliness does not deny the present for the sake of the future, either, but is valuable "for the present life and also for the life to come."

Verses 9–10—Notice how Paul never strays from the Gospel! For Paul, Christian living is *not* a separate topic from the saving Gospel of Jesus Christ, but it is an extension of it. Christians hope "on the living God, who is the Savior of all people," and this hope gives shape to the way we live our lives in this world.

The phrase "especially of those who believe" points to the gift of faith that God has given to you. Christ died for the sins of the whole world (John 3:16, 1 John 2:2), thus saving the world from death and damnation. Theologians often call this the Universal Atonement. But only those who believe, by the miracle of God, receive the blessing and benefit of God's saving work in Christ Jesus.

Verse 11—Now Paul flatly instructs Timothy to command and teach these things. For those who listen willingly and with repentant hearts, gentle teaching is sufficient. However, when gentle teaching will not suffice, commands must be used. This is especially true for false teachers with seared consciences and for their followers. There will be times when the pastor cannot convince his hearer by using gentle explanations. He will then have no choice but to state God's truth bluntly. Sheep will often willingly follow the voice of their shepherd, but the obstinate sometimes need to be driven along with a stick.

Verse 12—"Let no one despise you . . ." Timothy is young but not a recent convert. His place in the congregation has nothing to do with his age, experience, or any other personality trait. He is there because God placed him there. However, his divine call must not lead him to act as lord and ruler, but rather, he must "set the believers an example" in all that he does.

Verses 13–14—It seems that Paul wants Timothy to keep preaching and teaching as the greatest priorities in his pastoral work. Every other duty the pastor carries flows from these central tasks, be it the regular study of the Word or going out and visiting the sick.

Paul's mention of Timothy's gift might refer to a special power bestowed upon him, such as miraculous healing or the speaking of another language, as the apostles were certainly able to bestow these gifts. Luther believed the gift was "a power in doctrine and exhortation" (Luther's

Works, vol. 28, p. 330). But Paul might simply be referring to Timothy's ordination, which likely took place in a worship service that included the "prophetic word" of a sermon. It is not that the pastor receives some special bestowal of the Holy Spirit that other Christians do not receive! However, virtually every pastor will confess that, for all its labor and difficulty, it is a truly divine gift to be called to serve the church in this way.

Verses 15–16—The Word of God, along with the doctrine that arises from it, must never be neglected! All Christians must regard doctrine highly, and the pastor must be the most diligent of all, giving himself wholly to doctrine and to the Christian life that adorns it. By careful watch of his doctrine and his life, the faithful pastor will give none of his hearers an opportunity to fall away from the faith. They may fall for other reasons, but they must not fall because the pastor's lack of diligence incited them to it! The salvation that comes through the man's faithful preaching must never be destroyed by unfaithful living, for this will only breed contempt for the man, his pastoral office, and for the Word he preaches.

3 Caring for the Weaker Members of the Body of Christ (5:1–8)

Verses 1–2—Because the pastor adorns the Gospel with godly living, he shows both care and respect to God's people. His gentle care of his own wife and children (1 Timothy 3:2–5) will naturally find extension into the larger body of Christ. This applies especially to those in the congregation who might be more vulnerable than others.

Verses 3–8—The pastor must also act wisely. Some people will desire the lion's share of his attention. In a sinful world, many people will feign need for the sake of gain. Even members of a Christian congregation will be tempted to do so. The pastor will need to act wisely in his dealings with them, determining whether or not the need is real. Those who are truly needy will not be neglected, while those who fabricate needs will be required to repent. If help can be given from some other source, such as from family members, such help will be expected. Neglect of family—either those related by blood or those related by Baptism—is unimaginable! Such neglectors are worse than unbelievers.

Here Paul indicates that love for neighbor must be taught to Christians. Because sin remains even among Christians, they need to be instructed in such matters "so that they may be without reproach." The Gospel of our Lord Jesus Christ produces love for neighbor within your heart and mind, but, because of sin, the Law must show you the direction in which such love must now be exercised. In this case, Timothy's instructions will need to follow the Fourth Commandment: Honor your father and mother.

4 Do Not Tolerate Abuse of the Congregation's Care (5:9–20)

Verses 9–10—The list of widows is similar to today's shut-in list, though its members probably also received food provisions as well as communion visits. This list, however, was not to be used as a way for people to get free room and board in their old age. They must be well-established members of good reputation and piety.

Verses 11–16—Some of the younger widows might have pledged themselves to full-time service in the church and been placed on the list of widows in order to receive compensation for their work. But some later realized their desire to marry a second time and changed their minds about their work. Paul says that it is far better for them to make no full-time commitments to the church in the first place, so that they do not "incur condemnation for having abandoned their former faith."

The list of widows must not be used as an "early retirement" plan either. Anyone who is still able to marry and to work ought to do so, rather than soaking up congregational resources that could be better spent on the truly needy. Idleness among the younger widows will lead to gossip and other sins, so they must be kept busy.

Verses 17–20—Just as the recipients of the congregation's care and provision must not abuse the physical gifts they receive, so also must they not abuse the pastor, who distributes the greater gifts of God's mercy and forgiveness through the Word, through Baptism and through Holy Communion. He need not become rich, but he must be amply provided for. He must not be kowtowed to, but he must also not be shown disrespect or contempt. He must be protected against false accusation, and all things must be clearly established by multiple witnesses.

These verses in particular must be taken to heart by every pastor and every congregation. Sadly, there are many instances in which pastors act more like overlords than shepherds and many instances in which congregations act more like wolves than sheep. True repentance is needed here so that pastor and congregation may live together in love and humility under the forgiving Gospel of Christ.

5 The Pastor Loves and Cares for All in the Congregation (5:21–25)

Verse 21—Timothy has been placed into his work "in the presence of God and of Christ Jesus and of the elect angels," that is, God's holy angels. With all of heaven standing as witness, he must fulfill his office faithfully, showing God's people the same sort of patience, generosity, and love that God Himself holds toward them (as the congregation must likewise treat its pastor). If the pastor shows favoritism, he gives the impression that God shows favoritism, since he is God's representative and ambassador to the people.

Verse 22—The laying on of hands was used to ordain fellow pastors. Timothy must exercise restraint, not ordaining anyone until he is fully trained and examined. Such great care must be exercised even today, which is why congregations limit themselves to calling men who have been trained at recognized seminaries and have been examined by the leadership of the church.

Verse 23—Now Paul adds a bit of personal advice to his young friend. In ancient times, wine was used for medicinal purposes, among other things. By drinking a little wine, Timothy may find relief from his physical afflictions, which will make him more able to fulfill the day-to-day labors of his pastoral office.

Verses 24–25—God cannot be fooled! If some abuse the congregation's good graces (v. 13), lord their position over others (v. 21), or commit other sins, God will not be unaware. Those who live by faith will receive faith's reward; those who do not, will not.

6 Addendum Concerning Slaves (6:1–2)

Paul speaks specifically about slaves here, but his words may be applied to any number of situations in life. Just as slaves must respect their masters and not neglect them because they are brothers in Christ, so also must all those who are under another person's authority show love and respect, especially if the authority is a fellow Christian. God looks at all people equally: they have been washed clean in the blood of Christ, the sacrifice. Yet salvation does not erase the order in which we live—the order in which God created us to live. We observe good order and authority *all the more* because we believe.

Conclusion

This section of 1 Timothy charts the shape of the Christian congregation and those who serve it. Living repentantly together under the Word of God, each member of the congregation will not only occupy his or her place faithfully, but will also show love and respect for the others who occupy their God-given places. Life in the church does not consist of one person vying for position over or against another, but it consists of mutual repentance, genuine love for neighbor, and a piety that considers others as better than self. This is the same love that Christ Jesus showed for His church and for the world, and Christ's great, self-sacrificing love is what makes all of this possible.

Concluding Activities

Mention again the Enrichment Magazine and encourage participants to read it as part of their weekly study. Then distribute the study leaflet for the next session. Pray the following prayer:

O God, by the patient suffering of Your only-begotten Son You have beaten down the pride of the old enemy. Now help us, we humbly pray, rightly to treasure in our hearts all that our Lord has of His goodness borne for our sake that after His example we may bear with patience all that is adverse to us; through Jesus Christ, our Lord. Amen (*LW*, p. 125).

Join together in praying the Lord's Prayer, and then depart with the salutation:

L: The Lord be with you!

C: And also with you!

The Value of Faith above All Other Things

1 Timothy 6:3–21

Preparing for the Session

Central Focus

After outlining the way in which the pastor interacts with and cares for the members of his congregation (session 3), Paul now returns to the beginning of his Letter to Timothy, speaking the same sort of exhortation to faithfulness as he did in chapter 1 (session 1). Paul never allows himself or the church to stray too far from sound doctrine (that is, teaching)! In this summary section of his Letter, he calls upon his friend Timothy to focus again on the teaching he has received, to resist the temptations of wealth and to "pursue righ-teousness, godliness, faith, love, steadfastness, gentleness" (1 Timothy 6:11). Such labors, made possible by the Holy Spirit through His divine Word, will result in eternal treasures!

Objectives

That the participant, as a child of God and with the Holy Spirit's help, will be led deeper into the divinely given realizations that

1. the objectives, goals, and commitments of the world spell destruction for the Christian faith;

2. "the good confession" (1 Timothy 6:13) and strong doctrine are worth more than money, goods, family, friends, or anything else in the world;

3. God's people, no matter how they might struggle financially or otherwise, never are forgotten by God. He sees them, cares for them, and has established an eternal home for them in His presence.

Note for the small-group leaders: Lesson notes and other materials you will need begin on page 54.

For the Lecture Leader

Session Plan

Worship

Begin the session with the hymn printed in the study leaflet. Accompaniments are available in denominational hymnals, such as *Lutheran Worship* (refer to hymnal index). (Note: Concordia Publishing House has available *Every Voice a Song*, a 9-CD set of organ accompaniments for 180 hymns and liturgy. All the initial worship hymns in the LifeLight courses are included in this resource. It's especially helpful for mission congregations and small parishes. See the list of study resources on page 7.)

Prayer

Blessed Lord, since You have caused all Holy Scriptures to be written for our learning, grant that we may so hear them, read, mark, learn and take them to heart that by patience and comfort of Your holy Word we may embrace and ever hold fast the blessed hope of everlasting life, through Jesus Christ, our Lord. Amen (*LW*, p. 156).

Lecture Presentation

Introduction

Everyone has something they love most of all. Some become enticed by the love of wealth and devote themselves to accumulating "things." But they end up piercing themselves with grief (6:10). Others, by the power of God's Spirit and His Word, devote themselves to pursuing "righteousness, godliness, faith, love, steadfastness, gentleness" (6:11). These things, produced by God through the gift of faith, result in true treasures in "the future" (6:19).

1 Warnings about Material Wealth (6:3–10)

Verses 3–5—After repeatedly warning Timothy about the false teachers and the harm they will do, here Paul speaks a general indictment against them all: they are conceited, ignorant, and falsely motivated. This condemnation does not apply to those Christians who are still growing in knowledge of the Word and might not yet fully understand it. It applies to those who knowingly persist in errors for the sake of personal gain. Such teachers have been robbed of the truth and have become focused on personal gain. Perhaps some of today's televangelists fit this description, especially when they promise such things as healing and success if only you will send money to them.

The standard to which all teachings and teachers must be held is the "sound words of our Lord Jesus Christ and the teaching that accords with godliness." This points us to the Holy Scriptures, especially the Gospels, as the source of all teaching and preaching. If a man's message does not measure up to that which is written in the Scriptures, he is a false teacher. The result of his teaching will not be true unity in the faith, but sorrow in the church.

Accordingly, every Christian pastor and every Christian hearer has the duty and responsibility to do his or her part in studying carefully the sermons, Bible studies, devotional materials, and textbooks that are produced in the church. Each of these must be continually examined in light of the Word of God. Books ought not to be read and studied simply because they contain a few good ideas sprinkled amidst false teachings. Such books ought to be rejected entirely and replaced by those that are fully faithful to the divine Word. Many books are published and printed today not because of their faithfulness to the Word of God but because of their popularity. These things serve no benefit to the church but only become "a means of gain."

Verse 6—Paul now balances "gain" (v. 5) with the "great gain" created by godliness and contentment. Godliness is nothing other than the life of faith, created by the Gospel of our Lord Jesus Christ. Contentment realizes that God has provided me with all I need, and therefore I shall be satisfied with these things. Such divinely given realizations spell "great gain" for the Christian because they eliminate the need for competition with others, accumulation of materials, or any other such activity that requires constant attention and worry. God through Christ promises to care for each of His children, as surely as He cares for the lilies of the field and the birds of the air (Matthew 6:26–30). Worry expresses doubt bordering on unbelief, while contentment expresses trust in such promises from God.

Verses 7–8—A simple reality check will help restore the right perspective for those who have committed themselves to financial gain rather than the great gain of godliness and contentment: you can't take it with you! As Job realized, so may every Christian likewise pray, "Naked I came from my mother's womb, and naked shall I return. The Lord gave, and the Lord has taken away; blessed be the name of the Lord" (Job 1:21).

Verses 9–10—The desire to become rich all too easily becomes a full-time mental preoccupation. Such pursuits gratify the desires of the flesh for a short while, but then they quickly lead to "many senseless and harmful desires." Just as a drug addict will need more and more drugs to remain satisfied, those whose hearts are set on the accumulation of wealth cannot be content with a small fortune. They will want a larger one, then an even larger one after that. An all-consuming interest in money "develops vengeance, anger, envy" (Luther's Works, vol. 28, p. 371) and all sorts of destructive impulses. Simply think about the frequent news stories that highlight the misfortunes of those who win millions in the lottery. Such people usually end up bickering with relatives, going to court, losing their friends, and in misery rather than happiness.

Money is not the root of evil, but the *love* of money is. For the pious and content Christian, money can be a great tool for serving the Lord and His church. When the individual becomes "eager for money" (NIV), focused on receiving rather than giving, faith and salvation get placed in jeopardy. Such people become pierced (literally, "pierced completely through") with grief.

2 Focus Your Attention on the Stuff of Faith (6:11–16)

Verse 11—Paul charges Timothy, the "man of God," to focus his attention on higher things than material wealth. Timothy must flee from such temptations in the same way he would flee a deadly disease or a roaring forest fire. Yet such beneficial things as righteousness and godliness must be pursued in the manner a hunter would pursue his prey: quietly, patiently, and with full concentration.

Such gifts as "righteousness, godliness, faith, love, steadfastness, gentleness" do not occur naturally in those who are born in sin. These things must come about only by the grace of God, whose Word is "at work in you believers" (1 Thessalonians 2:13).

As a replacement for pursuing financial gain, Paul offers this laundry list of much better pursuits.

- *Righteousness:* Because he mentions here both righteousness and faith, it would seem that the righteousness he is talking about is not the righteousness of faith. Otherwise, why would he later mention faith? Righteousness in this passage more likely refers to outward righteousness, by which we live a good and decent life before God and man. This righteousness does not save us, but it is one of the fruits of faith.

- *Godliness:* This is similar to righteousness, but it includes faithful worship. Another word for it would be *piety*.
- *Faith:* This is one of God's highest gifts, which not only trusts in the promises He speaks to us, but also produces fruit.
- *Love:* One of the first and greatest fruits of faith, this love is made possible only by God's prior love for us (1 John 4:19). This gift from God gives us a desire and willingness to serve Him in our daily lives and an ability to bear patiently with our neighbor.
- *Endurance:* Sometimes translated as "patience" (KJV), this gift gives the ability to wait upon the Lord's deliverance from the trials and struggles that so regularly afflict the Christian life.
- *Gentleness:* With this gift, we overcome our sinful, inborn desire for revenge and learn to commit all things to God's gentle care and guidance.

Verse 12—Against what must Timothy fight? He must fight against the influences of the false teachers, who seek to divert Timothy's congregation away from the Gospel. He must fight the temptations and plans of the devil, who continually assails Christ's church, hoping to destroy faith. Timothy must even fight his own desires, temptations, discouragements, and sins. He must also struggle and fight to proclaim the Gospel in its clarity and power so that no one may be misled.

Success for his struggle will not be found in his own labors, however. The only way rightly to fight is to "take hold of the eternal life to which you were called." Literally, Timothy (and we!) must "firmly grasp" or "clutch in the hand" the eternal life given to him by Christ. Notice how God is the first actor: He called Timothy to eternal life, gave him the gift of faith, and made him His child. Now Timothy grasps that which already grasps him; now he clutches the gift for which God took hold of him.

Verses 13–14—With the words "in the presence of God," Paul now places Timothy under oath, charging him with a deep responsibility to the church. Timothy must never divert from the faith! Not only is his eternal salvation at stake, but so also is that of his hearers (recall 1 Timothy 4:16). The tasks of preaching God's Word and administering His gifts to the church must not be lightly undertaken, even by the seasoned veteran of the pastoral office. Each day, the pastor's labors must be undertaken with repentance and renewed faith, with careful study of the Word, and with fervent prayer that God will never allow any departures from it. For that matter, we ought to pray this way both for ourselves and for our pastor.

By mentioning Christ's good confession before Pontius Pilate, Paul evokes images of judgment and condemnation. As Jesus promised, "If the world hates you, know that it has hated Me before it hated you" (John 15:18). Timothy's good confession and "sound doctrine" (1 Timothy 1:10) will not win him many friends in this world. But as the next verses indicate, Timothy and we do not concern ourselves with living our lives before the world so much as we concern ourselves with living faithfully before God Himself.

Verses 15–16—The divinely bestowed endurance and gentleness pursued by the man and woman of God will enable each to stand firm until "the appearing of our Lord Jesus Christ" (v. 14). Even when it seems that the whole church is in uproar and that all Christian labors have come to naught, each pastor and Christian may look forward with confidence to the Last Day, which "[God] will display at the proper time." God is not unaware of the fight! He carefully watches and guards His tender flock, and He will gather us up into His eternal sheepfold at exactly the right time.

In view of God's sustaining power, Paul launches into a hymn of praise. He is "the King of kings and the Lord of lords." No one will ever overcome Him or defeat Him; no enemy can breach the walls of His kingdom; not one of His faithful people will ever find themselves outside the reach of His saving arm. The great hymn of the Reformation comes to mind:

> Though devils all the world should fill,
> 	All eager to devour us,
> We tremble not, we fear no ill,
> 	They shall not overpow'r us.
> This world's prince may still
> 	Scowl fierce as he will,
> He can harm us none,
> 	He's judged; the deed is done;
> One little word can fell him. (*LW* 298:3).

3 Living on Earth with a View to Heaven (6:17–21)

There are two summaries in the last section of this Letter. Verses 17–19 summarize the material covered in this *LifeLight* session, and verses 20–21 summarize the entire Letter.

Verses 17–19—There is no sin in being rich, and Paul certainly does not want Timothy or the church to draw the conclusion that Christians must be materially poor on earth in order to gain the riches of heaven. The love of money causes all sorts of evil (v. 10), not money itself. Wealthy Christians simply ought to consider themselves as having been given a larger responsibility to love their neighbor, meeting the church's needs where others are unable to do so. Riches used wrongly do very little for the individual, other than lead into temptation. But riches do much in serving the neighbor! Those materials given to the service of the church need not be considered a loss either. Generosity, prompted by faith in Jesus, leads to eternal treasures and "that which is truly life."

At various times in the life of the church, some people have theorized that Christianity ought to take the form of socialism, in which all possessions are supposedly held in common and no one has anything more than anyone else. But financial differences between Christians are actually God's gift to the church! By faith, rich Christians live Christlike lives, "not to be served, but to serve" (Matthew 20:28) and to give generously to the poor whether or not the poor seem to deserve it. The poor also learn the grace of receiving good gifts without opportunity to repay—which is exactly how the church lives in God's grace. Thus, rich and poor in the church become living models of the life-giving Gospel, using their very lives to proclaim to the world the undeserved grace that is given in Christ.

Verses 20–21—By way of final exhortation, Paul tells Timothy to carefully guard the sound teaching of the church, according to the Scriptures. Without sound doctrine, nothing else matters! Without faithful teaching, true love becomes impossible and all other matters of church life—fellowship, acts of charity, and the like—become useless. False teaching, no matter how appealing it might sound, will lead only to a departure from the saving faith.

Conclusion

"Grace be with you." Paul frequently ends his Letters with such statements as this. The grace of God that has been shown to us in Christ Jesus is the fountain and source of our life in the church. We never outgrow our need for this grace but continually return to it through daily repentance and faith. Such faith prompts every good deed done in Christ, performed by rich and poor alike, for the love of neighbor and the praise of God.

Concluding Activities

Distribute the study leaflet for the next session. Pray the following prayer:

Direct us, O Lord, in all our doings with Your most gracious favor, and further us with Your continual help that in all our works begun, continued, and ended in You we may glorify Your holy name and finally by Your mercy obtain eternal salvation; through Jesus Christ, our Lord. Amen (*LW*, p. 125).

Join together in praying the Lord's Prayer, and then depart with the salutation:

L: The Lord be with you!

C: And also with you!

Faith in the Midst of Hardship

2 Timothy 1:1–2:13

Preparing for the Session

Central Focus

Paul wrote this Letter while imprisoned in Rome (2 Timothy 1:16–17). Feeling lonely and abandoned, the apostle greatly desired to see his beloved Timothy again (2 Timothy 1:4), but he had also begun to think that he would likely die for the faith before such a visit could be made. Thus, while Paul cherished his warm memory of Timothy's "sincere faith" (2 Timothy 1:5), he wrote his friend a last will and testament, outlining the most important things that he wants Timothy to know and to believe. He calls upon Timothy to persevere in teaching the Gospel in a pure and unchanged form, even if such teaching should result in hardships endured for the faith (2 Timothy 2:3).

Objectives

That the participant, as a child of God and with the Holy Spirit's help, will be led deeper into the divinely given realizations that

1. Paul in his inspired Letter calls all Christians to faithfulness to the pure Gospel, no matter what hardships they may endure as a result;
2. Christ saved us and called us to a holy life because of His own purpose and grace, and not because of any good thing we could say or do;
3. the Gospel of our Lord Jesus Christ gives both courage and faith to God's people, with the result that they may face their hardships and struggles without fear but in the confidence that God will surely fulfill all His promises in Christ Jesus.

Note for the small-group leaders: Lesson notes and other materials you will need begin on page 57.

For the Lecture Leader

Session Plan

Worship

Begin the session with the Invocation, followed by the hymn printed in the study leaflet. Accompaniments are available in denominational hymnals, such as *Lutheran Worship* (refer to hymnal index). (Note: Concordia Publishing House has available *Every Voice a Song*, a 9-CD set of organ accompaniments for 180 hymns and liturgy. All the initial worship hymns in the LifeLight courses are included in this resource. It's especially helpful for mission congregations and small parishes. See the list of study resources on page 7.)

Prayer

Blessed Lord, since You have caused all Holy Scriptures to be written for our learning, grant that we may so hear them, read, mark, learn and take them to heart that by patience and comfort of Your holy Word we may embrace and ever hold fast the blessed hope of everlasting life, through Jesus Christ, our Lord. Amen (*LW*, p. 156).

Lecture Presentation

Introduction

Paul wrote his First Letter to Timothy while he was on the road preaching the Gospel to the nations. This Second Letter, written several years after the first, comes from the prison in Rome. Paul desires to see Timothy again but has begun to think that he shall die for the Gospel before Timothy can arrive. Therefore, the last and most important things the apostle would like to say to his friend must be committed to writing. Some scholars have even called this Letter Paul's last will and testament "in which he bids Timothy preserve the apostolic Gospel pure and unchanged" (Martin Franzmann, *The Word of the Lord Grows*, CPH, 1961, p. 161).

1 Greeting and Fond Memories (1:1–5)

Verses 1–2—This Second Letter begins almost exactly as the first began, with Paul identifying himself as an apostle of Christ Jesus. He does not hold this position because of his family pedigree, his personal characteristics, or even his high training. Paul is an apostle "by the will of God according to the promise of the life that is in Christ Jesus." Paul was sent to the nations to proclaim God's promise of life, and now in his last days he must cling to the same life-promise he proclaimed to others. Setting a godly example for all Christians in the face of impending death, Paul now focuses his own attention on the promise of eternal life that is his by the resurrection of the Lord Jesus Christ.

Verse 3—With plenty of time to think and to write, Paul especially remembers Timothy, whom he might even have considered his successor and theological heir. Thankfulness to God remains central on Paul's mind because he knows that the Word will not be bound (2 Timothy 2:9) but will continue to spread forth through the world despite the apostle's imprisonment and death. Apostles die; preachers come and go; the Word remains forever. Even here in prison, Paul's joy burns more brightly in the realization that Timothy and others carry onward the faithful work that Paul and others once began.

Verses 4–5—Christians give one another great joy and confidence. Timothy arouses Paul's faith by his own "sincere faith," which had been passed to him from his mother and grandmother. The sad memory of Paul and Timothy's separation is sweetened by the realization that Timothy is absent with a purpose, doing the work that God had given him to do. This work is the good fruit of faith, produced by the living and active Word that now does its work in Timothy.

2 A Call to Faithfulness (1:6–10)

Verses 6–7—With an eye toward the evidences of Timothy's faith, Paul calls upon his friend not to become a complacent or lazy pastor, but to "fan into flame" the gift that was given to him through the laying on of Paul's hands. Perhaps this laying of hands refers to Timothy's ordination into the pastoral office. Ordination into the pastoral office, of course, gives no special dispensation or outpouring of the Holy Spirit. The pastor's possession of the Holy Spirit is that of his Baptism, not his ordination. However, every pastor will surely agree that this labor itself is a divine gift! The duties of the office require careful attention, and the skills learned by the pastor require practice and use. Not only that, but the pastor must learn to balance courage with care. He must not be intimidated by those who oppose him wrongly, but he also must maintain a spirit of self-discipline and love, lest by his actions he dishonor his office. Through a conscientious pastoral practice, the pastoral gifts that God has given the man will become developed and mature.

Verses 8–10—What an ironic church in which we now live! Deeply shameful things such as cohabitation without marriage, homosexuality, and promiscuity are now tolerated to various degrees in many parts of Christianity, while those who live faithfully according to the Scriptures are made to feel ashamed of their position, as if they are too old-fashioned or judgmental! But Paul lauds and praises pious living. Do not be ashamed, says he, either of the Gospel or of those who live by it! Such people point not to themselves but to the God who saves them by His power in Christ Jesus.

The Greek word for "testify" is *marturion*, a word that later became associated with suffering for the sake of the Gospel. The martyrs lost their lives testifying "about our Lord." Paul's usage of the word does not yet carry this self-sacrificing overtone, but he closely associates the proclamation of the Gospel with Timothy's own physical participation in it: "share in suffering for the gospel." Such suffering is endured "by the power of God." This power—rooted in the death and resurrection of Jesus—comes to us by God's grace. The martyr/witness, faced with death, can take comfort in the fact that "our Savior Christ Jesus, [has] abolished death."

3 The Results of Such Faithfulness (1:11–18)

Verses 11–12—Timothy must take careful note! Paul's suffering is a result of preaching the Gospel. While he did not choose his place as an apostle and preacher, Paul moves forward in his God-given work with the confidence that no matter what loss he might suffer in this life for the Gospel, the eternal gifts given to him in Christ Jesus will remain unshaken. This great confidence gives Paul and every Christian a sense of shamelessness and joy, knowing that nothing can destroy the gifts that God has given to us in Christ.

Verse 13—Colleges and universities seek to foster creativity, individuality, and self-expression. Setting such things aside, the Christian seminary seeks to instill faithfulness in its graduates. Along with Timothy, every pastor—for that matter, every Christian—must hold faithfully the "pattern" or "model" or "outline" of sound teaching that Paul followed, himself having received it from Christ.

Verse 14—Ironically, the Gospel, which Paul also calls here "the promise of the life" (v. 1), must not only be kept (v. 13), but also guarded! That life-giving message God uses to protect you from all evil must also be protected from evil! Just as a nurse must keep careful watch over a patient's oxygen flow so that the oxygen may provide life to the patient, Timothy must keep watch over the Gospel so that it might not be impeded, diluted, or polluted by destructive false teachings. Such things spell not life, but death for the "patients," the Christians Timothy is given to guard and protect.

Verses 15–18—Deserted by nearly all his friends, Paul now has no consolation but the Gospel. Several friends have been helpful and "refreshing," but for the most part, Paul is now alone. This is not an expression of resentment toward others, but of resignation and acceptance of his situation. Paul provides no reason why his friends have left, and some possibly needed to fulfill their vocations and other responsibilities.

Worthy of note, however, is the great blessing given by those who were able to visit Paul in his loneliness. Would that every busy Christian find time to visit the sick and the elderly, if only for a few minutes on a monthly basis! Such visits of compassion and mercy, even short ones, do wonders for those who are "imprisoned," so to speak, by old age and frailty. Echoing our Lord's Sermon on the Mount (Matthew 5:7), Paul prays for an extra measure of divine mercy upon the friend who had been merciful toward him in his need.

4 Analogies Concerning Faithfulness (2:1–7)

Verse 1—Amid the labors of the Christian life in general and the pastoral office in particular, Paul exhorts Timothy to remain strong. He does not call Timothy to find inner strength, and he does not exhort Timothy to greater effort for the Kingdom. Rather, Paul points his friend to the life-giving, strength-bestowing Gospel as his source of strength.

Verse 2—Nor must Timothy remain alone in his work. To those who are qualified, Timothy should extend the right and responsibility of joining in the pastoral work that he himself received from Paul. This echoes what Paul wrote earlier in 1 Timothy 3:1–7 and 5:22.

Verses 3–4—Many people have heard the old saying" A picture is worth a thousand words." After outlining to Timothy (1) the great importance of the Gospel and (2) Timothy's role in both guarding it and proclaiming it, Paul now provides a series of word pictures to drive the point home for Timothy in a very compelling way. What he says applies to us, who are also called by God to share the Good News about Jesus with people.

The first word picture is that of a *soldier*: a combat-trained soldier remains focused on his calling and faithfully serves despites suffering. In the same way, Timothy must realize that suffering will be part of his vocation. Yet such things are willingly endured by those who are committed to something much greater than one's own personal comfort.

Verse 5—The second word picture is that of an *athlete*: athletic training is likewise a form of personal suffering, willingly undertaken. Not only that, but the athlete must also follow the rules imposed by others. In the same way, the Christian pastor is not free to pick and choose those things from the Scriptures that he likes the best and forget the rest. He must faithfully bring all of God's Word to bear in his work—even when faithfulness makes him personally uncomfortable. If he fails to do so, he could find himself disqualified.

Verse 6—The first two word pictures are a preaching of the Law, illustrating what Timothy ought to do in the office of the ministry. The third word picture is a sermon of comfort and peace: God will provide for you! Just as a *farmer* receives a share of the crops he raises, so also will Timothy find provision for himself in the preaching of the Gospel. This word picture will remind Timothy of what was written in the First Letter, "'You shall not muzzle an ox when it treads out the grain,' and, 'The laborer deserves his wages'" (1 Timothy 5:18).

This image of farmer and field is a wonderful picture of the pastor's work. The farmer really can do nothing more than plant seeds and protect them while they grow. The growth comes from God. In the same way, the pastor is also a planter/protector who waits upon the Lord to supply the harvest. Every Christian is called to help and support him in this blessed work. As Paul writes to the Christian congregation at Rome: "My brothers . . . you yourselves are full of goodness, filled with all knowledge and able to instruct one another" (Romans 15:14).

Verse 7—When Paul uses the word "reflect" (NIV), he indicates that he wants Timothy to do more than merely read this Letter, then set it aside. These important words need to be chewed and re-chewed, like a cow with her cud. As Timothy ruminates on what Paul has written, the divine Word will continue to work in his heart and mind, strengthening him for his daunting task.

This is a good way for every Christian to approach the Scriptures. As one old seminary professor described the reading of the Word, "Never . . . allow the words 'OF COURSE' be used" (Martin Franzmann, *Ha! Ha! Among the Trumpets*, CPH, 1966, 1994, preface). That is, the Christian must never approach the divine Word assuming that he or she already knows fully what is written. The Word is deeper than even the greatest ocean depth, and it cannot ever be fully plumbed or examined. Each adventure in reading the Word holds the promise of new and deeper understanding, which in turn renews and strengthens the baptismal faith.

5 The Faithful Christian Goes Only Where Faithful Jesus First Has Gone (2:8–13)

Verses 8–9—The Lord Jesus Christ, "risen from the dead," sends no one anyplace that He Himself has not already gone. Just as He suffered and rose, so also may we proceed forward into our own suffering, knowing that, by Baptism, we too shall rise. The knowledge that Christ rose up from the dead does more than inspire us to follow Him. Christ's resurrection ensures and promises our own resurrection, stripping death of all its terrors. Paul, believing that he is now on the verge of death, places his chains in proper perspective: though he is treated like a common criminal, the Word of God which saves him cannot be chained, but it will prove faithful to life everlasting.

Verse 10—In his Letter to the Philippians, written before 2 Timothy, Paul expressed a desire "to depart and be with Christ." (Philippians 1:23). Yet he concluded that it would be better for him to remain in this life, for the sake of the saints on earth. Here in 2 Timothy, Paul now expresses a similar thought: "I endure everything for the sake for the elect, that they also may obtain the salvation that is in Christ Jesus with eternal glory." Paul does not suffer to please God, for Christ already did that. Paul now suffers for the sake of the brethren, in order that they may (1) hear the Gospel of salvation, (2) be strengthened by Paul's faith and witness, and (3) console themselves that they too will be preserved by God through suffering.

Verses 11–13—Paul appears to quote an ancient Christian hymn, perhaps even one that Timothy's congregation regularly sang in worship. The entire focus of these lines is Christ Jesus. Just as a flock of sheep follows where its shepherd leads, so also will we Christians follow Jesus even through death into life.

The phrase "if we have died with Him" echoes Paul's declaration that "we were buried therefore with Him by baptism into death, in order that, just as Christ was raised from the dead by the glory of the Father, we too might walk in newness of life" (Romans 6:4). The Christian's resurrection from the dead on the Last Day is already a foregone conclusion for Paul—and for us! All that remains is the fairly small work of enduring faithfully, and this endurance itself is made possible only by the powerful and divine Word of Christ's Gospel.

Conclusion

As Paul now faces what he believes will be his own, final inclusion in Christ's suffering, he calls upon his dear friend and younger brother in the Lord to carry on the work that the apostle will leave behind. Timothy would likewise face hardship, as we will. But do not fear! Jesus Christ rose up from the dead. This resurrection now shapes and colors our work, including that of the pastor. The resurrection strips us of all fear and shame on account of sin and allows us to look boldly at all the best our enemies can offer, for "if we have died with Him"—which we already have in Baptism—"we will also live with Him" (v. 11) in eternity.

Concluding Activities

Make any necessary announcements. Then distribute the study leaflet for the next session. Pray the following prayer:

Almighty God, our heavenly Father, of Your tender love towards us sinners You have given us Your Son that, believing in Him, we might have everlasting life. Continue to grant us Your Holy Spirit that we may remain steadfast in this faith to the end and come to life everlasting; through Jesus Christ, our Lord. Amen (*LW*, p. 125).

Join together in praying the Lord's Prayer, and then depart with the salutation:

L: The Lord be with you!

C: And also with you!

Faith Put to Action in Life

2 Timothy 2:14–3:17

Preparing for the Session

Central Focus

Believing he is near death, Paul wrote this Letter to Timothy as a theological last will and testament, stressing to his younger friend the great need to remain faithful to "the pattern of the sound words" (2 Timothy 1:13) and the "good deposit" (1:14) that had been entrusted to him. Part of Timothy's faithfulness will require that he entrust others with the pastoral office. In his First Letter to Timothy, Paul outlined the qualifications for those who would become pastors (1 Timothy 3:1–7). Now, as he thinks about Timothy's work of entrusting others, Paul contemplates the sort of temptations and struggles these men will face as they undertake their labors.

Objectives

That the participant, as a child of God and with the Holy Spirit's help, will be led deeper into the divinely given realizations that

1. the Word of God, rather than "irreverent babble" (2:16), must remain at the center of the church's life and conversation;

2. those who wish to live piously according to the Word of God will be persecuted (2:12), even by people in the church who have "the appearance of godliness, but [deny] its power" (3:5);

3. the living Word of the Scriptures is not merely information, but it is the very power of God that actively guards and protects you against harm and danger.

Note for the small-group leaders: Lesson notes and other materials you will need begin on page 60.

For the Lecture Leader

Session Plan

Worship

Begin the session with the Invocation, followed by the hymn printed in the study leaflet. Accompaniments are available in denominational hymnals, such as *Lutheran Worship* (refer to hymnal index). (Note: Concordia Publishing House has available *Every Voice a Song*, a 9-CD set of organ accompaniments for 180 hymns and liturgy. All the initial worship hymns in the LifeLight courses are included in this resource. It's especially helpful for mission congregations and small parishes. See the list of study resources on page 7.)

Prayer

Blessed Lord, since You have caused all Holy Scriptures to be written for our learning, grant that we may so hear them, read, mark, learn and take them to heart that by patience and comfort of Your holy Word we may embrace and ever hold fast the blessed hope of everlasting life, through Jesus Christ, our Lord. Amen (*LW*, p. 156).

Lecture Presentation

Introduction

False teaching will always remain a clear and present danger for the church. If at any time God's Christians think that they are safe from such temptations, they are at the greatest risk for a fall! Yet God's Word, faithfully preached and confessed, is mighty and powerful. It shall not fail to guard and protect the Lord's beloved Christians against those things that would seek to destroy their faith.

1 The Dangers of False Teaching in the Church (2:14–19)

Verse 14—To whom does "them" refer in this verse? Probably not Christians, because this verse refers to them as "the hearers." Paul seems to be saying, "Keep reminding the *pastors* of these things" (see 2:2). The pastors must be reminded and warned not to "quarrel about words"—that is, they must not get into senseless arguments—because such senseless quarrels will only ruin the faith of the Christian hearer. The pastor must faithfully preach the divine Word instead, nourishing and preserving the Christian congregation with God's gifts, so that they may "obtain the salvation" (2:10).

Verse 15—Timothy and all pastors (along with all Christians) remain sinners, yet because Christ's crucified blood has set them free from sin and death, they need not be ashamed. In particular, they need not feel ashamed of their proclamation "Thus says the Lord" when they faithfully preach the divine Word. Such faithful preachers—indeed all Christians—will be opposed by the false teachers, by some of their hearers, and even by their own temptations, sins, and fears. All of these will marshal their efforts together to make the pastor ashamed of his office and his proclamation. Yet Paul insists, by the grace and power of the resurrected Christ, that faithful preaching is no point of shame. Such faithfulness produces a workman approved by God.

Verses 16–18—If a child walks around a puddle rather than through it, his feet will stay dry. If a Christian turns off radio or TV programs produced by false teachers, his or her mind and faith will be protected and preserved. If a pastor avoids "irreverent babble" and remains focused on his calling and his preaching, he will avoid spreading the dangerous, gangrene-like plague of deceptions, half-truths, and lies that already proliferate in the church.

Some of the worst falsehoods (or heresies) in the church are those that sound like they fit well into the Scriptures. Paul gives the example of Hymenaeus and Philetus, who were teaching that the resurrection of believers had already taken place—and there is a sense in which they were right, because Holy Baptism is a participation not only in Christ's death but also in His resurrection (Romans 6:1–7). However, the Scriptures also make it clear that the resurrection of all flesh is still in the future, on the Last Day.

Today's church likewise suffers under falsehoods that sound good to some people, but are clearly contrary to the Word of God. Such errors include the ordination of women (advocates claim that this is an issue of equality), the acceptance of homosexuality as an "alternative lifestyle" (advocates claim that this is an issue of love and acceptance), and even abortion (advocates claim that this is an issue of freedom). Yet all of these things, along with many more falsehoods, can destroy the Christian faith in the same way that gangrene destroys a human body. Therefore Paul calls upon his friend Timothy to remain focused on God's Word and to remain firmly secure in it.

Verse 19—Against every error and heresy that might creep into the church, "God's firm foundation" that He created for us in His Word shall stand firm. Even if everyone else in creation turns their backs upon us who live faithfully according to the Scriptures, God will not forget us! He gave His Son to save us, and He certainly will not abandon us now.

2 The Pastoral Office Is Not about Personal Position, but about Faithfulness (2:20–26)

Verses 20–21—Paul's discussion of the false teachers raises the question, "Why are there such people in the church?" He answers in the form of an analogy: some household items are used for "dishonorable" purposes (for example, vessels for collecting garbage and body waste). The false teachers are like dishonorable household vessels. It is necessary to have them (see 1 Corinthians 11:18–19!), even if they must be avoided. Such teachers help God's people understand faithful teaching by clearly illustrating *unfaithful* teaching. Those who avoid such dishonorable vessels will become "a vessel for honorable use, set apart as holy, useful to the master of the house." Perhaps we could summarize Paul in this way: If you want to remain a centerpiece on the dinner table, stay away from the septic tank!

Verses 22–24—Several other temptations assail the faithful preachers (and hearers) of God's Word, including the sensual passions of youth. Such desires do not serve the church, but only the physical flesh.

Paul also warns that the pastor will be unable to argue anyone into the faith. God's Word is not mere information that we must try to convince people to believe, but it is a divine power, miraculously producing faith in those who hear it. If you end up arguing about this or that aspect of God's Word, quarrels, resentments, and other hard feelings will result. If you point to a Bible passage and say, "This I believe, and here is why," you have made the good confession (1 Timothy 6:12–13), allowing God's powerful Word to do its work.

Verses 25–26—The pastor will not speak only to those who willingly listen and agree with him either! He must also speak with those oppose him, confessing the faith as gently to them as he does to his friends and fellow believers. In the face of opposition, he makes his good confession knowing that God gives the gift of repentance (that is, God creates both sorrow over sin and faith in Jesus Christ's death and resurrection for the forgiveness of the world's sins). The individual Christian has no power to save; only God's powerful Word is able to lead one's opponents to their senses and deliver them from unbelief.

3 False Teachings and Sins Will Grow Worse as the Last Day Approaches (3:1–9)

Verses 1–5a—The labor of making the good confession, however, will not be light duty! The world becomes increasingly evil with every passing day and has continued on this downward course since the earliest days of sin and rebellion in the Garden of Eden. Every sin imaginable will become increasingly welcomed and accepted by the mass of humanity. These sins, as horrible as they are in the eyes of God, will become "standard operating procedure" in society. Even today, many Christians can look back over the course of their lives and see how society has morally declined since the days of their childhood. Yet in these verses, Paul is not only talking about life in the world. He is talking about life in the church! In the last days, terrible things will happen in the church: people will trade faith and piety for all sorts of sins, taking on an outward form of godliness, but having no faith in Christ.

Christians confess the faith with the realization that they cannot make the world—or the church—"a better place." They can, however, continue to "have mercy on those who doubt; save others by snatching them out of the fire; . . . show mercy with fear, hating even the garment stained by the flesh" (Jude 22–23).

Verse 5b—"Avoid such people." Paul does *not* call upon pastors and laypeople to become monks and nuns, hiding away from the world! He insists that we have nothing to do with those who claim to be Christian yet do not live by faith and piety. This command mirrors his First Letter to the Corinthians, in which he writes,

> I wrote to you in my letter not to associate with sexually immoral people—not at all meaning the sexually immoral of this world, or the greedy and swindlers, or idolaters, since then you would need to go out of this world. But now I am writing to you not to associate with anyone who bears the name of brother if he is guilty of sexual immorality or greed, or is an idolater, reviler, drunkard, or swindler—not even to eat with such a one. (1 Corinthians 5:9–11)

Christians must avoid such "christians" and "pastors" who claim to be part of the church but live counterfeit lives.

Verses 6–8—False teaching does its best work when it preys upon those who are weak and vulnerable. Paul gives the example of certain women who struggled with doubt and sin, only to have the false teachers exploit those weaknesses and lead them away from the faith. Just as Jannes and Jambres (Pharaoh's sorcerers who opposed Moses, Exodus 7:11) acted in a spectacular way in their opposition to the truth, so will the false teachers offer many convincing proofs and arguments to support their lies.

Verse 9—Yet because faithful Christians love and protect each other against such things, those who are weak will be rescued by the strong (Timothy among them). When Timothy gently and patiently makes the good confession based on the clear Word of God, the foolish errors of the false teachers will become plain, and those who were once tempted to follow them will be turned back to the true faith again.

4 Through All, God's Word Will Preserve and Protect (3:10–17)

Verses 10–11—God protects His people through His Word, through the remembrance of Baptism, through Holy Communion, and even through the mutual consolation of the brethren. Paul himself endured the very things he sees in Timothy's future. Yet Timothy can rest content in the knowledge that God shall deliver him for the sake of Christ as surely as He delivered Paul.

Verses 12–13—And not Timothy alone! "All who desire to live a godly life in Christ Jesus will be persecuted." The word "all" is a warning even to us, as well as a comfort and promise that God will continue to guard and protect His Christians even today.

Verse 14—What is the important thing for us today? It is that same thing that was important for Timothy centuries ago: that we continue in what we have learned from the Scriptures, not allowing ourselves to be diverted from faith in Christ's death and resurrection for the forgiveness of our sins.

Verses 15–16—The concluding verses of this chapter are essential knowledge for every Christian. Here Paul proclaims that the Scriptures are not merely "divine information" that people hear, think about, and decide whether or not they want to believe. The Scriptures are the very voice of God, the life-giving power that raises the dead and sets the creation itself into motion. God's Word does not teach wisdom, but it bestows the gift of wisdom "for salvation through faith in Christ Jesus."

Verse 17—The powerful Word of God goes beyond the creation of faith. God's Word also produces good works in you. Just as a seagoing vessel gets fully supplied for its trip, or a traveler's wagon carried everything necessary for the journey, so also does God's Word supply "all things that pertain to life and godliness" (2 Peter 1:3). In fact, God's Word itself *produces* good works in you! No Christian can say, "I believe; I am simply unable to do good works." Instead, every believer can happily confess, "Christ saved me by His death and resurrection, washing me clean in His blood and giving me the gift of eternal life. Because He has also, by His Spirit, created faith in me, everything I now do pleases Him. My waking and my sleeping are good works; my daily tasks are good works; my speech and conduct are also good works in His sight. Because God has caused His Word and Spirit to dwell within me, He produces in me such things as are pleasing to Him, for the sake of His Son, Jesus."

Conclusion

Luther summarized 2 Timothy in this way:

> This epistle is a farewell letter, in which St. Paul exhorts Timothy to go on propagating the gospel, even as he has begun. This is quite necessary, since there are many who fall away; and false spirits and teachers keep springing up all around. Therefore it is incumbent upon a bishop [pastor] always to be alert and to work at the gospel.
>
> But [Paul] prophesies especially, in chapters 3 and 4, concerning the perilous time at the end of the world. It is then that a false spiritual life will lead all the world astray, with an outward show, under which every sort of wickedness and wrong will have its fling. Sad to say! We now see this prophecy of St. Paul all too amply fulfilled in our clergy [and our church]. (Luther's Works, vol. 35, p. 389)

Even so! God's powerful and life-giving Word assures and promises every Christian that He shall guard and protect that which He has created. Let all the world and even the false saints align against the faithful! He shall yet preserve His remnant for the sake of Christ.

Concluding Activities

Make any necessary announcements. Then distribute the study leaflet for the next session. Pray the following prayer:

Almighty, merciful, and most gracious God, we earnestly implore You to turn the hearts of all who have forsaken the faith once delivered to Your Church, those who have wandered from it or are in doubt or temptation through the corruption of Your truth; mercifully visit them and turn them again that in singleness of heart they may take pleasure in Your Word and be made wise to salvation through faith in Jesus Christ, our Lord. Amen (*LW*, pp. 125–26).

Join together in praying the Lord's Prayer, and then depart with the salutation:

L: The Lord be with you!

C: And also with you!

Guard against Those Things That Attack Faith

2 Timothy 4; Titus 1

Preparing for the Session

Central Focus

In the last chapter of 2 Timothy, Paul summarizes the most important things he wants Timothy to remember and to do. His message to Titus (probably written between the two Letters to Timothy) is essentially the same as his message to Timothy: the pastor must serve faithfully! Thus we will see that the life of the Christian faith, lived by pastor and by laypeople alike, remains basically the same no matter where or when it is lived. Even today, sin still afflicts God's people; false teachers still spread their lies; Jesus' blood still gives forgiveness and life; God's Word and Spirit still preserve and protect those whom He has called to be His own.

Objectives

That the participant, as a child of God and with the Holy Spirit's help, will be led deeper into the divinely given realizations that

1. God's Word will faithfully guard and sustain all God's saints in their time of need, as it did for Paul in what he believed were the waning days of his life;
2. even if friends and family should abandon God's saints, the abiding presence of the Holy Spirit in the Word shall remain (which is part of the reason why faithfulness to the Word is so essential);
3. that God calls all pastors and all Christians to the same sort of faithfulness to which He calls Timothy and Titus.

Note for the small-group leaders: Lesson notes and other materials you will need begin on page 62.

For the Lecture Leader

Session Plan

Worship

Begin the session with the Invocation, followed by the hymn printed in the study leaflet. Accompaniments are available in denominational hymnals, such as *Lutheran Worship* (refer to hymnal index). (Note: Concordia Publishing House has available *Every Voice a Song,* a 9-CD set of organ accompaniments for 180 hymns and liturgy. All the initial worship hymns in the LifeLight courses are included in this resource. It's especially helpful for mission congregations and small parishes. See the list of study resources on page 7.)

Prayer

Blessed Lord, since You have caused all Holy Scriptures to be written for our learning, grant that we may so hear them, read, mark, learn and take them to heart that by patience and comfort of Your holy Word we may embrace and ever hold fast the blessed hope of everlasting life, through Jesus Christ, our Lord. Amen (*LW*, p. 156).

Lecture Presentation

Introduction

Hermann Sasse, a Lutheran theologian who confessed the faith in Germany during and after World War II, once described faithfulness to God's Word as "the lonely way." Even when it seems that the entire world and church have turned away, the "lonely" Christian perseveres faithfully unto the end. Lonely faithfulness is Paul's lot in 2 Timothy 4, as well as the position that likely awaits both Timothy and Titus in the future. Yet such loneliness of the faith in this life will be answered by joy and peace in the resurrection of all flesh and by unity with God in heaven.

1 Timothy's Entire Responsibility in a Nutshell (4:1–5)

Verses 1–2—The omniscient God (Psalm 139:7–9) who promises always to be with His people (Matthew 28:20) now stands as witness to Paul's command, "preach the word." Paul cannot verify that Timothy will faithfully do that which he is given to do, but He who judges "the living and the dead" shall hold all preachers accountable. Yet this is not cause for fear! Those who preach faithfully have already been given the gift of faith, which clings to Jesus' death and resurrection for salvation.

The command to preach the Word is perhaps the simplest summary of every pastor's duty and responsibility. Of course, he must also administer the Sacraments, admonish the erring, comfort the repentant, visit the sick and imprisoned, and live a life in keeping with the Gospel, all "with complete patience and teaching." But these duties all flow naturally from the kernel of his duties: preach the Word. Would that all pastors and congregations took this message to heart! Too many pastors become diverted by ancillary tasks (such as chairing committees, overseeing fund-raisers, motivating building projects, etc.), and too many congregations lay great expectations on the pastor in this regard. Yet for him to focus on these lesser things is for him to take away from the central, highest, and most precious duty of his office: preaching the Word.

Verses 3–4—Essentially Paul says to Timothy and to all preachers and hearers of the Word today, "Make the most of your preaching while you can! Soon, pure doctrine and faithful preaching will no longer be tolerated by many people. They will choose preachers who will not preach but will only stroke egos and prattle about nonsense. While you still have the opportunity, preach the Word!"

Verse 5—Then Paul goes on: "Even when sound and faithful preaching is no longer tolerated in the church, do not panic, dear Timothy! Realize even now that things will be difficult for you in the future, just as they are now difficult for me, and calmly face whatever your Lord will allow you to suffer. Flight from your office will not be an option, but do the work of an evangelist (that is, a preacher of the Gospel) no matter what sort of reaction you get from your hearers. Just as the captain of a ship must remain at the wheel no matter how harsh the weather becomes, so also must you discharge the duties of your ministry, no matter what storm or tempest may assail you and your congregation."

2 Paul Is Near the End of His Earthly Days (4:6–18)

Verses 6–7—Having warned Timothy of future difficulties in the pastoral office, Paul now reflects on the culmination of his own preaching, which has resulted in imprisonment. Death is near, and Paul faces it without regret, knowing that he has "kept the faith," not only believing in Jesus Christ for eternal salvation, but also calling others to do the same.

Verse 8—As Paul contemplates his death, however, he does not think merely in terms of going to heaven to be with Jesus. Paul's greatest hope and desire is in the Last Day, in the return of His Christ in glory, and in the resurrection of all flesh. Paul longs for the Lord's reappearing with all who have preceded him in the faith, and in the resurrection Paul shall receive "the crown of righ-teousness," which the Lord Jesus Christ has prepared for His apostle (and for all believers) in His suffering, death, and resurrection.

Verses 9–13—Despite Paul's confidence of faith, he is still a man, and a sinner at that. Loneliness has begun to set in, and he longs to see his beloved Timothy yet again before he dies. Little else is available to cheer him by way of human comforts. Paul's friends have either abandoned him (Demas) or have been required to go elsewhere to preach the Word (Crescens and Titus). Only Luke remains, and his presence is a welcome gift.

These verses provide a rather intimate picture of the apostle who elsewhere appears so mighty and fearless before the church and the world. Paul must now rely on the compassion and ministrations of his friends. The mention of his cloak points to those same human needs that the apostle shares with all people, yet his ongoing desire to write and to preach outweighs even these considerations: "bring . . . above all the parchments."

Verses 14–15—Paul's self-reflection brings to mind Alexander, who had done some sort of harm to the apostle. But Alexander will not incur Paul's wrath; God will take care of it. Paul and all Christians may rest in the knowledge that the Creator and Redeemer of the universe truly sees all of His children and all of their sufferings. All injustices done to the Lord's beloved people will at last be repaid.

Timothy, however, will still need to contend with Alexander after Paul has entered the Lord's rest. Alexander's preaching opposes the faithful preaching of the church, but it appears to have been influential. Timothy must act with great caution, because Alexander is no friend!

Verse 16—Even while Paul holds no personal enmity against the false preacher Alexander, who openly opposed him, he cannot help but feel the insult and injury incurred by his friends who failed to support him when he first appeared in the Roman courts. His prayer that their sins may not be held against them probably does not indicate that he hopes God will forgive them—God in Christ has already forgiven much greater sins! But Paul hopes that other Christians will not resent his friends' desertion in his time of need. It will be easy for many Christians to say, "You should have remained with Paul in his need! I certainly would have done so!" But Paul knows the weakness of the flesh. He holds nothing against his friends, and he hopes that others will likewise treat these people with forbearance.

Verses 17–18—Even in the midst of loneliness, Paul straightens and confesses, "The Lord will rescue me from every evil deed." The Lord preserved him at his first defense, keeping him from perishing in the arena, and the Lord shall continue to preserve him. Paul does not claim that he will never die; he only confesses faith that the Lord will "bring me safely into His heavenly kingdom." In all things, whether Paul lives or Paul dies, the Lord's name shall receive glory eternally, for the Lord is faithful and He cannot fail. "Lord, may this be our prayer and goal for life with You!"

3 Last Greetings to the Church (4:19–22)

This Second Letter to Timothy closes with some personal greetings to a few Christians in Ephesus. Last details are provided to Timothy concerning other workers whom he knew and loved. Those few Christians who remain with Paul send their greetings, but the greatest and most profound greeting is saved for last: "The Lord be with your spirit. Grace be with you."

4 Introduction to Titus

Luther called this Letter "a kind of epitome and summary of other, wordier epistles" (Luther's Works, vol. 29, foreword). Here Paul states in a very tight form the whole of the Christian life, which is begun and finished in Christ Jesus. After treating the pastoral office, its duties and conduct (ch. 1), Paul goes on to describe how Christians in other vocations likewise live by faith (ch. 2). This life is rooted in Baptism (ch. 3), through which God in His mercy has called His people away from the passions and pleasures of the world.

5 Greetings to Titus (1:1–4)

Verses 1–3—Where Paul used only the word "apostle" in his Letters to Timothy, here he adds the word "servant" or "slave" to his self-description. Paul does not speak or act for himself. He is a slave of God, preaching for "the faith of God's elect and their knowledge of the truth." (The word "elect" is simply a synonym for "Christian.") Such faith and knowledge, which rest on the promise of eternal life, produce godliness here in the present.

That Jesus is the divine Word that creates faith and gives knowledge comes to the church through Paul's preaching, along with the preaching of the prophets, the other apostles, and the four evangelists, Matthew, Mark, Luke, and John. Through their testimony read and preached in the church, God continues even to this day creating faith, godliness, and the knowledge of eternal life.

Verse 4—The phrase "common faith" carries the idea of [Greek] *koinonia*, or divinely created fellowship. Even when separated from each other, Paul and Titus, along with all faithful Christians, share a common bond of trust in Jesus. This bond cannot be achieved by our own labors or efforts, but it results only from the miraculous work of God. This is why true Christian worship remains—and must remain—so focused on Christ and His Word.

6 Titus's Job Is Not Much Different from Timothy's (1:5–16)

Verse 5—At a time that is not mentioned in the Book of Acts, Paul and Titus must have begun preaching on Crete, a Mediterranean island not far from modern Greece. Paul's duties required that he continue traveling, but the church in Crete still needed careful attention. So he left Titus behind, giving him the duty of training and installing pastors to carry on the work that the two companions had first begun.

Verses 6–9—In order to remind Titus what sort of man qualifies for the office, Paul briefly summarizes the same sort of material that he wrote in his First Letter to Timothy (3:1–7). He uses the words "elder" and "overseer" to describe the office, which are words that indicate a position of authority over others. However, the pastor does not use his authority abusively, as the kings of the world would do (Matthew 20:25–26). His is a position of authoritative servitude, which would be an oxymoron in any place other than the church. Above all, the pastor must hold the Christian faith according to the Scriptures, because the Word of God is the only tool at his disposal by which he can both encourage the faithful and oppose the unfaithful.

Verse 10—Just as Paul warned Timothy about those who "will depart from the faith by devoting themselves to deceitful spirits" (1 Timothy 4:1), he also warns Titus about "many who are insubordinate." Of special difficulty are the circumcision group, who believed and taught that Gentile converts to Christianity must first be circumcised. Because forgiveness, life, and salvation are free gifts from God, there must be no additional requirement added!

Verse 11—One of the greatest afflictions that God's Christians must suffer, even today, is the false preaching that you must first do something in order to be saved. Not only is this misrepresentation of the Christian faith "upsetting whole families," but it also burdens consciences. Far better that we preach the blessed news that Christ has died for the sins of the entire world and that He fully and freely forgives everyone in His blood. Such preaching instills the gift of faith in the heart and mind of the hearer, entirely before he or she is even able to do anything to amend his or her sinful life!

Verses 12–14—Here Paul uses a line from the Cretan poet Epimenides as a way of condemning those "who are insubordinate . . . of the circumcision party" (v. 10). When agreeing with Epimenides, Paul is not condemning the entire island of Crete, but only those false teachers who mislead for the sake of dishonest gain. Because their work is rooted not in the faith but in belly service, such liars must be sharply and publicly rebuked, lest their temptations spread through the whole congregation.

Paul is not throwing away Jesus' command that we quietly approach our erring brother, one-on-one (Matthew 18:15). Titus is not facing a matter of individual sin but a matter of public proclamation that threatens to destroy the church. Decisive action must be taken, and quickly, in order to prevent the wholesale destruction of faith among those who believe.

Verses 15–16—False teachers are not merely mistaken! They have committed themselves to a course that contradicts the Word of God and sound teaching. Therefore, nothing about them is good or beneficial. They must be entirely avoided, like disease-ridden clothing or infectious waste. "They are detestable, disobedient, unfit for any good work."

Paul's words here will likely provide a stinging rebuke to those Christians and congregations who today make use of the reading materials, evangelism programs, and hymnals of publishers who do not hold to a Christ-centered, Bible-based confession of the faith. Paul is not in the business of "taking the best and leaving the rest" when it comes to the preaching of the church. Rather, he wants only faithfulness on the part of God's preachers and His people. Those who knowingly head in other directions will bring the church nothing good or profitable for life and salvation.

Conclusion

It may seem odd that Paul so strenuously preaches that the powerful Word of God must be guarded and protected against falsehoods. After all, it is God's Word! Isn't God able to take care of Himself? Of course He is!

Consider these analogies: A scuba diver carefully guards his oxygen tube because he knows that this is the way life-giving air gets delivered to his lungs. An astronaut on a space walk will pay close attention to his tether, knowing that this lifeline will both keep him from floating helplessly into space and lead him back again to the safety of the shuttle. In the same way, those who love Jesus will keep, guard, preserve, store up, and pay careful heed to His Word because they know that Jesus comes to them through His teaching, makes His abode with them, and comforts them with His forgiving presence. For this reason, Paul exhorts Timothy, Titus, and all pastors and Christians to carefully keep God's Word, that we may always receive from it the gifts of forgiveness and life.

Concluding Activities

Make any necessary announcements. Then distribute the study leaflet for the next session. Pray the following prayer:

Almighty God, our heavenly Father, of Your tender love towards us sinners You have given us Your Son that, believing in Him, we might have everlasting life. Continue to grant us Your Holy Spirit that we may remain steadfast in this faith to the end and come to life everlasting; through Jesus Christ, our Lord. Amen (*LW*, p. 125).

Join together in praying the Lord's Prayer, and then depart with the salutation:

L: The Lord be with you!

C: And also with you!

Faithful Teaching Produces Faithful Living

Titus 2–3

Preparing for the Session

Central Focus

In Titus chapter 2, Paul teaches Titus how he must preach to Christians, applying to various positions and stations in life certain exhortations and responsibilities that pertain to each. These Christians must hear the Law, gently preached to them, so that they will know what it means to live in accord with sound doctrine. This preaching of the Word will lead them to the forgiving Word of the Gospel, through which "the grace of God has appeared, bringing salvation for all people" (2:11). This grace first came to them in God's gift of Baptism, as Paul explains in chapter 3.

Objectives

That the participant, as a child of God and with the Holy Spirit's help, will be led deeper into the divinely given realizations that

1. godly and pious living results naturally from sound teaching;
2. such godliness and piety comes from God and His grace, made possible in us through the Holy Spirit, who was given in Baptism;
3. forbearance and patience toward our neighbor's temptations and sins become easier when we remember our own former foolishness and acts of impiety.

Note for the small-group leaders: Leaders notes and other materials you will need begin on page 65.

For the Lecture Leader

Session Plan

Worship

Begin the session with the Invocation, followed by the hymn printed in the study leaflet. Accompaniments are available in denominational hymnals, such as *Lutheran Worship* (refer to hymnal index). (Note: Concordia Publishing House has available *Every Voice a Song*, a 9-CD set of organ accompaniments for 180 hymns and liturgy. All the initial worship hymns in the LifeLight courses are included in this resource. It's especially helpful for mission congregations and small parishes. See the list of study resources on page 7.)

Prayer

Blessed Lord, since You have caused all Holy Scriptures to be written for our learning, grant that we may so hear them, read, mark, learn, and take them to heart that by patience and comfort of Your holy Word we may embrace and ever hold fast the blessed hope of everlasting life, through Jesus Christ, our Lord. Amen (*LW*, p. 156).

Lecture Presentation

Introduction

Here Paul instructs Titus to preach the Law to Christians, exhorting each to live a life that reflects sound teaching, no matter who they are or what place they hold in the congregation. But then Paul continues his Letter with the precious and life-giving Gospel, proclaiming that God's grace in Christ Jesus has come "for all people" (2:11).

1 Living in Accord with Sound Doctrine (2:1–10)

Verse 1—Paul places the word "you" in an emphatic position, stressing that Titus has the responsibility to preach and teach what is in accord with sound doctrine. He cannot pass this duty off to another, and he certainly cannot assume that others will step up and do it if he should fail to do so. Titus is the pastor. Ultimately, he shall be held responsible for the public teaching of the congregation. He must teach what is in accord with sound doctrine, whether or not anyone listens or lives accordingly.

Verses 2–5—Because the older men will naturally be looked upon as examples and role models, it is imperative that they—above all others—live according to sound teaching. The older women must likewise act reverently, bearing in mind that the younger women learn from their example in both word and deed. The training of younger women will include devotion to home, family, and daily tasks, lest idleness give them opportunity to sin.

Pious living reflects the sound teaching of the church, giving no one the opportunity to blaspheme God by saying, "What kind of religion is that? Look at the way those people live—they believe and teach fine things but live as if their words had no meaning! Why should we take seriously the message of the Scriptures if the Christians will not?"

Verses 6–8—The young men of the congregation will likewise need to be taught self-control. As Titus himself is young, he will be able both to exhort the men verbally and to set an example for them by his own life through doing what is good. Titus's life and conduct actually has a double edge: not only must he set the example for the other young men of the congregation, but he also is the one of the congregation's most visible Christians in the community. As a public representative of what the church believes and confesses, Titus's life most especially gets scrutinized. It is not that he must live perfectly, but he *must* live penitently, with integrity and faithfulness of speech.

Verses 9–10—Paul preaches even to those in positions of servitude, who might otherwise be deceived into thinking their pious living is not all that important to the congregation. Christians—even those who seem to be in the lowliest positions—always get noticed.

Paul adds another dimension to the life of faith: "So that in everything they may adorn the doctrine of God our Savior." Paul means that godly and pious living makes the Gospel of Jesus Christ even more beautiful and gives praise to Him.

2 God's Grace Is the Foundation of Piety and Godly Living (2:11–15)

Verse 11—Even after such a gentle preaching of the Law as we see in these verses (no one is explicitly condemned for their sins, but only exhorted toward pious living), Titus's congregation will not help but feel the weight of their sins and failures. What Christian could ever claim that he or she has lived and believed and spoken perfectly? Who cannot think of instances in which their words or actions might have scandalized someone or might have discouraged someone? The consolations of the Gospel must always follow after the preaching of the Law, and Paul points Titus and his congregation to Jesus' cross and resurrection: "The grace of God has appeared, bringing salvation for all people."

Verses 12–13—In His powerful Word, God graciously proclaims the salvation that Christ won for us. This proclamation works a change in our hearts and minds. After the gift of faith gets planted and takes root, God's grace continues to do its good work in us. It teaches Christians to resist temptation and "worldly passions" and to exercise the sort of self-control and restraint that complements the Gospel. But God is not a lecturer who stands before the class wagging His finger and saying, "You must do this or that." Rather, He acts like the gymnastics coach or swimming instructor whose hands-on training helps and guides the student through each action. Our new life in Christ is the good fruit that God Himself produces in us through His Word and Spirit, by which He chastises, comforts, trains, and instructs.

Verses 13–14—The church's great expectation for the future, "the appearing of the glory of our great God and Savior Jesus Christ," finds its foundation in the past: "who gave Himself for us." Christ's self-sacrifice provides every Christian with (1) redemption, that is, the ransom-payment price paid to God for the debt we incurred through our sin and (2) purity, that is, the cleansing of heart and mind and conscience so that we will no longer feel the weight of our own condemnation.

Verse 15—Having offered this brief summary of God's gracious action in Christ, along with a description of the sort of life that God's people must live in keeping with God's grace, Paul now returns to the thought he expressed in 2:1. *You* teach in this manner, Titus! *You* exercise the authority of your pastoral office to encourage, rebuke, and teach.

3 God Gives Forgiveness and Rebirth in Baptism (3:1–11)

Verses 1–2—Paul also recognizes that some people will despise Titus and his preaching. This is why he concludes the previous verse with "Let no one disregard you" (2:15). How shall Titus do that? He shall remind the people to be subject to rulers and authorities. Certainly God's people must be subject to the civil government, but the context of this Letter indicates that Paul also wants them to be subject to the authority of the pastoral office.

Christians regularly hear sad stories about pastors who seem to lord their position over the congregation, or of congregations who decide they do not like their pastor trying to get rid of him by cutting his salary, ignoring his preaching, and other measures. Both extremes contradict the Word of God. Paul insists here that the pastor's relationship to the congregation must be rooted in the Word. When the pastor preaches the Word unfaithfully, of course he must be rebuked and corrected and even opposed, especially if he will not listen to sound doctrine. But when the pastor speaks faithfully and when he endeavors to shape his own life according to the Gospel, the congregation ought to thank God for the gift they have received in this man. This applies even if the people do not particularly care for the pastor as an individual. The best relationship between pastor and congregation is one of mutual humility and mutual repentance, powered by the Gospel.

Verses 3–5a—In thinking about the sort of life the people of God must live, Paul reflects on their former lives, before their divinely created metamorphosis. We all were once "foolish, disobedient, led astray, slaves to various passions and pleasures." None of us deserves the mercy shown to us by Christ, yet we are nevertheless redeemed and purified by His blood. This redemption and purity cannot help but instill patience and forbearance toward others, especially those who struggle with temptation and sin.

Verses 5b–7—Talk of redemption leads to talk about Baptism, which is called the road by which mercy comes to us (Luther's Works, vol. 29, p. 81). In the baptismal font, God works both rebirth (new life where there was once death) and renewal (replacing the old with the new). In Baptism, God pours out His Holy Spirit, by whom we are made able to believe. In Baptism, we become heirs of God, promised to receive the great, eternal riches He has stored up for us in Christ Jesus.

Verse 8—So while Titus must stress pure doctrine and holy living, he must do so within the context of his congregation's Baptism. "I want you to insist on these things" because Baptism is the way holy living is made possible, through the giving of the Holy Spirit. By virtue of their Baptism, God's people "devote themselves to good works" because God has already declared them good, right, and holy.

Verses 9–11—The pastor's faithful preaching and the congregation's remembrance of Baptism "are excellent and profitable for people" (v. 8). It is much better to be preoccupied with such things as these rather than to engage in foolish controversies. The person who sidesteps the sound teaching of God's Word poses a danger to the congregation's health and peace. If such a divisive person will not repent of his or her loveless action toward God's people, discipline must result. It is not that the congregation passes judgment! "He is self-condemned." The congregation's act of excommunication simply becomes a formal recognition of what the divisive individual has done for himself or herself. Such rebels are not "thrown out"; their self-exclusion simply becomes accepted by all.

This idea of self-condemnation ties into what Paul earlier preached to different groups in the congregation. It is also exceedingly applicable to today's church, especially for those congregations that have people who insist on remaining listed on the membership rolls but refuse to worship, ignore the Ten Commandments, and live as if God does not matter. They have excluded themselves from the inheritance God once gave them in Baptism. Essentially, they have thrown away their Baptism. Their own actions condemn them, even while they demand that they be called Christian.

4 Closing the Letter (3:12–15)

Verses 12–14—Winding down this brief summary of Christian faith and life, which is rooted in Baptism, Paul now turns to some personal items. A couple of capable men are on the way to relieve Titus of his duties, so that he may come to Paul. Two other travelers, Zenas and Apollos, will be passing through to some unmentioned designation. Their needs must be met. By helping them, Titus will demonstrate to the rest of the congregation the sort of generosity and openhandedness that the Gospel creates. Such lessons must be continually taught so that no one will mistakenly think that the Christian generosity of others is a license to laziness or that the freedom that God has created for them in the Gospel means that they themselves now have no brotherly responsibilities. Love for neighbor, rooted in the Gospel, is what this Letter is all about. It is fitting, therefore, that Paul would close with an exhortation that the Christians show love for their neighbors by living productive lives, each as he or she as able.

Verse 15—As the life of the church is that of a family, those who are with Paul sent greetings to Titus and the rest of the congregation. Warm regard for fellow Christians, that is, "those who love us in the faith," characterizes the piety of the church. There is no "I love you but I do not like you" nonsense. Brotherly love greets the brothers in love—even those whom we perhaps have never met.

Conclusion

Luther's brief summary of the Letter to Titus will makes a good conclusion for the present discussion. Luther writes,

> We have this epistle, which is brief but is filled with very good instruction and admonitions, so that there is almost nothing in the church that is not treated here. Let everyone see to it that he abides in the Christian message that Christ has been given for us, and in [works of] love that are not in vain. . . . He who wants to be a good Christian must urge that Christ be preached in all purity. (Luther's Works, vol. 29, pp. 89–90)

Concluding Activities

Make necessary announcements. Then distribute the study leaflet for the next session. Pray the following prayer:

Almighty God, give us grace that we may cast away the works of darkness and put upon ourselves the armor of light, now in the time of this mortal life, in which Your Son Jesus Christ came to visit us in great humility, that in the last day, when He shall come again in glory to judge both the living and the dead, we may rise to the life immortal; through Jesus Christ, our Lord. Amen (*LW*, p. 125).

Join together in praying the Lord's Prayer, and then depart with the salutation:

L: The Lord be with you!

C: And also with you!

Love for Neighbor Arises from Faith

Philemon

Preparing for the Session

Central Focus

Paul repeats the phrase *in Christ* throughout this short Letter, revealing that our treatment of our neighbor is rooted in nothing other than the Gospel. Paul's request that Philemon welcome back the escaped slave Onesimus provides us with the opportunity to contemplate our own treatment of our neighbor within the context of God's grace shown to us *in Christ*.

Objectives

That the participant, as a child of God and with the Holy Spirit's help, will be led deeper into the divinely given realizations that

1. even though the Letter to Philemon does not expressly discuss Christian teaching, the Gospel of Christ forms the background for the things that are written here;
2. the Gospel is not merely for our Sunday morning worship, but it permeates every aspect of our life in this world;
3. our treatment of our neighbor is rooted in the gracious treatment Christ has given us through His death and resurrection.

Note for the small-group leaders: Leaders notes and other materials you will need begin on page 67.

For the Lecture Leader

Session Plan

Worship

Begin the session with the Invocation, followed by the hymn printed in the study leaflet. Accompaniments are available in denominational hymnals, such as *Lutheran Worship* (refer to hymnal index). Note: Concordia Publishing House has available *Every Voice a Song*, a 9-CD set of organ accompaniments for 180 hymns and liturgy. All the initial worship hymns in the LifeLight courses are included in this resource. It's especially helpful for mission congregations and small parishes. See the list of study resources on page 7.

Prayer

Blessed Lord, since You have caused all Holy Scriptures to be written for our learning, grant that we may so hear them, read, mark, learn and take them to heart that by patience and comfort of Your holy Word we may embrace and ever hold fast the blessed hope of everlasting life, through Jesus Christ, Your Son, our Lord. Amen (*LW*, p. 156).

Lecture Presentation

Introduction

In this Letter, Paul pleads with the slave owner Philemon on behalf of Onesimus, the escaped slave. While many Bible scholars note that it contains no explicit discussion of Christian teaching, Martin Franzmann summarized this Letter's importance in this way:

> One of the valuable insights that [the letter to Philemon] affords is that there is no line of cleavage between the official Paul and the person Paul; for both, life has one content and one meaning: "For me to live is Christ." (*The Word of the Lord Grows*, CPH, 1961, p. 128)

In a day when Christians are tempted to view their Sunday morning worship as separate and unrelated to the rest of their week, Paul's Letter calls us to view our lives as a whole before God. We daily live *in Christ,* to borrow a repeated phrase from the Letter (vv. 8, 20, 23). Jesus Christ is, in fact, the foundation upon which this Letter is written. As we work our way through it, we will keep our eyes and ears open for allusions and overtones pointing us to Him.

1 Greeting with Thanksgiving to God (1–7)

Verses 1–2—Although he is literally imprisoned, possibly in Rome or Ephesus, Paul describes himself not as a prisoner of the Romans, but as "a prisoner for Christ Jesus." He does not consider his life his own, to be used as he chooses. Rather, he believes himself obligated to Christ, not only imprisoned for Christ's sake, but also devoted entirely to Christ, His Lord and Master, "doing the will of God from [his] heart" (Ephesians 6:6).

Paul addresses his Letter to Philemon, Apphia, presumably Philemon's wife, and Archippus, who was perhaps a pastor. The loving relationships reflected in the words "our brother," "beloved fellow worker," "sister," and "fellow soldier" (see also vv. 23–24) presuppose the mighty work of the Gospel. Paul regards Timothy, Philemon, Apphia, and the others mentioned in this Letter as his family, friends, and co-workers. He does so because of the bond they share *in Christ.* This deep bond extends also to "the church in [Philemon's] house." (The Christians met in homes because the Jewish synagogues generally no longer welcomed them, Acts 17:1–5).

Verse 3—Variations on this greeting are used in every one of Paul's Letters, both at the beginning and at the end. In each case, these words form "Gospel bookends" that set the entire Letter and all of its contents within the context of God's grace and peace shown to us in Christ. Even the harsh things that Paul sometimes writes to the churches must be heard within this context. Everything in the church begins and ends with divine grace, including the deeply personal relationships that develop between Christians. Even though Philemon is a personal Letter, it was most likely intended to be read from the pulpit like Paul's other Letters. Paul begins with God's *grace and peace,* and every appeal that he will make to Philemon refers back to these things

Verses 4–7—Many of Paul's Letters also include expressions of thanksgiving to God for the people to whom Paul writes. In this case, Paul is thankful for "your love and . . . faith that you have toward the Lord Jesus and all the saints," speaking not only about Philemon's faith and love, but including all of the others as well. This Letter addresses a topic specific to Philemon (and probably Apphia), but there is still a churchly aspect to it. Christians are not merely individuals in a crowd. They are all members together of the body of Christ (1 Corinthians 12:27). Philemon's life and actions impact the church that meets in his home as well as the entire church on earth.

Why would Paul thank God for the faith and love shown by these Christians? Well, faith and love both come only from God. Faith is not something we give to God, but something God gives to us (Ephesians 2:8; Romans 10:17; 2 Peter 1:1). Likewise, "we love because He first loved us" (1 John 4:19). Our very ability to believe in God and to love our neighbor is a divine gift! This gift, displayed in our lives, gives "joy and comfort" to our fellow Christians, just as it refreshed Paul's heart and "the hearts of the saints."

In verse 6, Paul warms up to the main purpose of his Letter. However, some translations may cause a misunderstanding of this verse. Paul does not speak so much of the *exercise* of faith, but he prays that the *fellowship* or *participation* ("koinonia" in the Greek) of the Christians' faith, one with another, will produce a deeper knowledge of every good gift they have received in Christ. The very act of participating together in Holy Communion, for example, will deepen the participant's understanding of that great, divine gift.

2 A Brotherly Plea (8–20)

Verses 8–9—Paul could have commanded Philemon to welcome back his escaped slave, and Philemon likely would have complied, if for no other reason than respect for Paul. But Paul is not in the business of abusing his pastoral authority. He intercedes for Onesimus, just as Christ intercedes for us before the Father (Romans 8:34; 1 John 2:1). Paul is a preacher of Christ crucified, not a demanding boss. He would much rather pull on Philemon's heart strings, not only appealing to Philemon's faith but also to his own advanced age and the presence of his chains.

Verse 10—Onesimus became Paul's son through Paul's preaching of the Word. We have no idea how these two could have met, especially since Onesimus was a fugitive and Paul was under house arrest. But our heavenly Father provided for their miraculous meeting, the result of which was salvation for a slave.

Verses 11–13—Paul very well could have simply claimed "finders keepers" and never written to Philemon.

Instead, he uses his own life to demonstrate the same faith-generated generosity that he requests of Philemon. Paul does not cry, "Do as I say," but he lives, "Do as I do." In this way he becomes a living proclamation of God's grace and forgiveness in Christ. This demonstration of love is not something given only to apostles, either, but here Paul marks a trail that may be followed by every Christian: Not only do we speak the faith, but we live it in humility and in love for neighbor, demonstrating with our very lives the Gospel of reconciliation and peace.

Verse 14—Paul is a keeper of the fourth commandment, not usurping one man's authority over another because "there is no authority except from God" (Romans 13:1). Bearing in mind that slavery in the Roman world bears little comparison to the brutal American form with which most of us are acquainted, we need not think it an offensive thing that a man would have God-given authority over a slave. Many slaves during this time were regarded as members of the household, receiving gentle treatment and respect from their masters. Paul does not consider the Roman form of slavery a matter of degradation or inhumanity, but he declares that "Each one should remain in the condition in which he was called" (1 Corinthians 7:20). Paul will not bypass Philemon's authority, because he wants Philemon to act as a Christian. Philemon may be expected to use the opportunity to act generously toward those whom God has given him.

Verses 15–16—Now Paul turns theological, offering Philemon a good Bible-based way of thinking about his slave's escape. Rather than viewing the separation as loveless thievery, perhaps Philemon should look at Onesimus as a player in God's providence. If Onesimus had not escaped, he would not have repented and returned to a greater relationship with Philemon. Onesimus is no longer merely a slave, but he is a "brother in the Lord" (NIV).

These two amazing and important verses not only open our eyes to the way we ought to view our Christian neighbor—putting the best construction on everything—but they also echo the Gospel of our Lord Jesus Christ. We, like Onesimus, were once separated slaves who have now been rejoined to our rightful master, our heavenly Father. As Paul mediated the reunion between Philemon and Onesimus, Jesus Christ in His death and resurrection likewise mediated the reunion for us with our heavenly Father, so that we may be received back to His household with a much greater status than ever before.

Verse 17—Paul now reaches the height of his intercession on the slave's behalf. He does not ask Philemon to consider Onesimus, but rather, he points Philemon to himself, asking Philemon to welcome Onesimus "as you would receive me." This, too, echoes of the Christ who intercedes for us before His Father, asking God to welcome us not because of who we are, but because of who Christ is and what He did for us on the cross.

Verses 18–19—Aside from the intercession, Paul also offers a Christlike payment for the debt that Onesimus cannot pay. Onesimus likely stole some of Philemon's property in his escape, and Paul pledges to cover the debt himself. Yet again we have a wonderful allusion to the Gospel of Jesus Christ, who redeemed us "not with gold or silver, but with His holy, precious blood and with His innocent suffering and death" (Small Catechism, Explanation of the Second Article). The generosity Christ showed to us, emptying Himself even unto death, is the motor and drive shaft of the generosity we now show to others. What good are all our earthly possessions, if not for the love of neighbor? For this reason, we gladly labor for our pay, using our income to serve children and spouse, family, friends, and each needy Christian God sends our way.

Verse 20—After every appeal to Philemon's faith, weaving allusions to the Gospel throughout his Letter, Paul now speaks on a personal note. Philemon's generosity in welcoming back Onesimus will not only benefit the slave, but will also refresh Paul's heart. Paul's life, with its constant sufferings, had plenty of opportunity to see greed, lovelessness, and malice in action. Paul will profit from Philemon's generosity to Onesimus because he will see the Christian faith in action—the very faith he has dedicated his life to preaching throughout the world. Philemon here will once again have opportunity to give Paul, likely his own spiritual father, "much joy and comfort" (v. 7).

3 Closing Remarks (21–25)

Verses 21–22—Paul obviously believes that Philemon will not only grant his loving request, but will also prevent any hard feelings from entering into their relationship. Hospitality and generosity will remain as ever. Paul's confidence stands in stark contrast to today's tendency. We often let our neighbor's impositions upon us destroy our love and regard for him! Yet Christ's forgiveness and forbearance do a great work in us: they create forgiveness and forbearance toward our neighbor.

Philemon could very well have felt himself justified in demanding Onesimus back with full reparations. He could have felt offended at Paul's interference. He could also have granted Paul's request but then vowed never to have anything to do with Paul or Onesimus again. But Paul does not believe things will go so badly. He assumes faith on Philemon's part. That is, he assumes that his neighbor will act piously and accommodate every one of his requests in Christ—not because Philemon must, but because Philemon loves Christ.

Verses 23–24—Paul's companions share his love for Philemon and his family, and they send their greetings. Even though they may have met only once or twice during the missionary journeys, the fellowship created for them "in Christ" creates a lasting bond and affection for their fellow saints.

Verse 25—The Letter ends as it began—with "the grace of the Lord Jesus Christ." By this grace, we live together as brothers, sisters, and fellows in Christ. By this same grace this Letter to Philemon teaches Christ's ongoing care not only for those Onesimuses who fall and must be restored, but also for those Philemons who must make life-altering decisions that impact both themselves and others around them. "The grace of the Lord Jesus Christ" permeates the whole of our life together.

Conclusion

As this is the last session in this *LifeLight* series, I encourage the class to reflect back on this Letter during the coming week, focusing especially on those verses that create overtones or echoes that bring to mind God's work for us in Christ. These overtones include but are not limited to the following:

- By Christ's death and resurrection for us, we who were once "runaway slaves" are now received as sons (v. 10).
- Christ intercedes for us before the Father, as Paul did for Onesimus (vv. 8–11, 17).
- God's reconciliation to us in Christ enables our reconciliation one to another (v. 12).
- We who were once separated from God because of sin are now brought near again (vv. 15–16).
- Christ willingly paid the full penalty for every debt we incurred (vv. 18–19).

Concluding Activities

Give the group opportunity to voice prayer requests, particularly those that arose out of an examination of their own lives in the light of studying Philemon. After praying together about these concerns, invite the class to write down the five points listed in the conclusion to the lecture and to contemplate them in the coming week. Make any necessary announcements, including whatever plans there may be for the next LifeLight course.

Join together in praying the Lord's Prayer, and then depart with the salutation:

L: The Lord be with you!

C: And also with you!

Small-Group Leaders Material

To a True Son in the Faith

1 Timothy 1

Preparing for the Session

Central Focus

Paul begins his Letter to Timothy by focusing on the vital importance of sound doctrine (that is, teaching) for the Christian church. The Gospel is essential to the church's life, for it gives the divine gift of faith even to blasphemers and persecutors and violent men (1 Timothy 1:13). Yet the Law is also good, and it must be used properly (1 Timothy 1:8). The church's faithful teaching of the pure Word of God—both Law and Gospel—must never become mixed with false teachings, because such falsehoods will only lead people away from the faith.

Objectives

That the participant, as a child of God and with the Holy Spirit's help, will be led deeper into the divinely given realizations that

1. in its earliest days, the church already struggled with false teachers;
2. both God's Law and His Gospel remain essential to the individual Christian's faith and life;
3. when God's Word is no longer taken seriously in the church, but gets replaced by "vain discussion" (1 Timothy 1:6), Christians will inevitably make "shipwreck of their faith" (1 Timothy 1:19).

For the Small-Group Leader

Small-Group Discussion Helps

Day 1 • 1 Timothy 1:1–2

1. (a) Paul identifies himself as an "apostle of Christ Jesus." This title was conferred on him by the command of God and of Jesus Christ. The twelve disciples—*and Paul*—were distinguished as *apostles* because they were eyewitnesses of the resurrected Christ. (b) Having Paul's imprimatur as well as his God-given credentials spelled out at the beginning of the Epistle would no doubt be a great asset for Timothy, especially if his teaching was challenged by others at Ephesus. Given Timothy's relative youthfulness, it seems likely that some would be inclined to doubt his authority. Paul's name and title, however, would serve as the authorization for Timothy to teach and carry out his duties as Paul's personal representative.

2. (a) Answers will vary. We often speak of hope in the sense of "wishful thinking," (e.g., "I hope it doesn't rain"; "I hope all goes well.") (b) When hope is equated with Jesus Christ, however, it conveys the idea of absolute certainty and confident expectation. In Jesus we have a "living hope" (1 Peter 1:3) made certain by His resurrection from the dead. This hope endures even through suffering and "does not put us to shame" (Romans 5:1–5). (c) As time permits, let volunteers share their answers.

3. Here and in other places Paul describes Timothy as his "true child in the faith." Paul was Timothy's spiritual father. For his part, Timothy enjoyed Paul's complete trust and respect. There was no doubt a strong bond of love and affection between these men.

4. Timothy came from the city of Lystra in Asia Minor (present-day Turkey). His mother was a Jewish believer. His father, however, was a Greek. Timothy was highly regarded by his fellow Christians. Before starting his travels with Paul, Timothy was circumcised by Paul. This was done not because circumcision was necessary for salvation, but to facilitate their mission work among Jews who still held to the ceremonial laws of the Old Testament.

5. (a) God's name is invoked by Paul two times in these verses. The name of Jesus is mentioned no less than three times. (b) More than mere redundancy, the repetition of the divine names underscores that what follows in this Epistle—the teaching, the admonitions, the life-giving Gospel itself—comes neither from Paul nor Timothy but from the God these men are privileged to serve. Whatever "confidence" and "sufficiency" (2 Corinthians 3:4–6) Paul and Timothy may possess comes from the Lord.

Day 2 • 1 Timothy 1:3–7

6. Certain men in Ephesus were teaching false doctrines. Rooted in myths and genealogies, these teachings were the source of much controversy.

7. At its heart, false doctrine of any kind is a corruption of God's truth. The author of all false doctrine is ultimately the devil. He is "the father of lies" and "there is no truth in him" (John 8:44). Paul's words in Galatians chapter 1 underscore the apostle's passion for keeping the Gospel of Christ pure. Paul speaks a harsh word of condemnation for anyone who preaches "a different gospel." False doctrine not only hinders the mission of the church, but may also lead the child of God to wander from the truth and, ultimately, to lose his or her faith in Christ.

8. (a) Answers will vary. Among the many myths at work in our culture is the myth that abortion is nothing more than "a woman's right to choose," or that God's gift of sex can find expression apart from God's gift of marriage, or that "all roads lead to heaven" since "we all worship the same God," or that God only expects me to do my best and will reward my good works with eternal life. (b) Answers will vary, but all rationales for accepting such myths are ultimately rooted in human sinfulness.

9. (a) Words like "humility," "gentleness," "patience," "love," and "peace" characterize the manner by which false teaching should be confronted and extinguished within the church. (b) These verses depict a body of believers that is mature in the faith, able to discern truth from error, and built up in the love of Jesus Christ.

Day 3 • 1 Timothy 1:8–11

10. (a) Broadly speaking, the purpose of the Law is to show us our sin. (b) While the Law is a good gift from God, it can neither save us nor justify us before God. Its power is limited. The Gospel, however, carries with it the power of God for salvation.

11. (a) When the human heart is overpowered by a supercharged dose of the Law, despair is often the result, as in the case of Judas. There is a hopelessness that results when God's requirements and our failure to meet those requirements is constantly pounded into us. The other possibility is that we delude ourselves into believing that *we can* measure up to God's requirements by our own efforts and works. Like the Pharisees of Jesus' day, we can take on a certain spiritual arrogance that leads us to pray, "God, I thank You that I am not like other men" (Luke 18:11). (b) Without the Law, the awareness of our sin diminishes. We no longer view our sins with alarm, nor do we see them as breaking God's commands. Instead, our sins become "mistakes," "lapses in judgment," and so on. Without the Law, we come to view our sins as "no big deal," and our need for a Savior from sin likewise becomes "no big deal."

12. The "ungodly" are not atheists, but, rather, those who have replaced the one true God with idols of their own choosing. This term, while somewhat general, does connect with "You shall have no other gods before me" (Exodus 20:3). The "unholy" and "profane" take what is holy and make it profane. "You shall not take the name of the LORD your God in vain" (Exodus 20:7) leads us to recognize the holiness of God's name and forbids us to use it carelessly or uselessly. "Those who strike their fathers and mothers" together with "murderers" brings us to the commandments that say "Honor your father and your mother" (Exodus 20:12) and "You shall not murder" (Exodus 20:13). "The sexually immoral" and "men who practice homosexuality" fall under "adultery." "Enslavers" can be understood as those who take someone captive, in effect "stealing" another person and breaking the commandment against stealing. "Liars" and "perjurers" are guilty of transgressing the commandment against false testimony.

13. Answers will vary. Make sure that the participants understand that the Gospel is essentially the Good News about Jesus—that we are saved eternally because of Christ's perfect keeping of the Law and His innocent suffering and death for us on the cross. His resurrection from the dead is the guarantee of our own resurrection on the Last Day. All this is a free gift of God's grace, which the child of God receives through faith.

Day 4 • 1 Timothy 1:12–17

14. Saul was present at the stoning of Stephen and "approved of his execution" (Acts 8:1). He sought to destroy the church. He imprisoned the people of God. While Saul prepared to enter the city of Damascus, still breathing threats against the disciples, the Lord Jesus appeared to Saul. The Lord's question, "Why are you persecuting me?" (Acts 9:4), shows that Saul's sinful wrath was ultimately directed against Jesus Himself.

15. 1 Timothy 1:15 tells us that Jesus Christ came into the world to save sinners. 1 Timothy 3:1 reveals that anyone who sets his heart on being an overseer (pastor) desires a

noble task. 1 Timothy 4:9–10 shows that God is the Savior of all men, freely offering His salvation to all people.

16. (a) Paul confesses that he is the "foremost" of sinners. (b) Answers will vary.

17. Answers will vary.

Day 5 • 1 Timothy 1:18–20

18. These three passages, respectively, show that we fight against the devil (1 Peter 5:8–9), this dark world (1 John 2:15–17), and our own sinful nature (Romans 7:18–25).

19. In verse 19, Paul notes that some have rejected and shipwrecked their faith. In 1 Corinthians 10, Paul uses the example of Israel's disobedience as a warning for Christians. "Therefore let anyone who thinks that he stands take heed lest he fall" (v. 12). These passages show that God's gracious gift of salvation *can* be lost.

20. (a) If Jesus was *not* physically resurrected, then *we* shall not be physically resurrected—and, most terrible of all, "[our] faith is futile and [we] are still in [our] sins" (1 Corinthians 15:17)—lost forever. (b) The false teaching actually destroyed the faith of some.

21. According to these passages, church discipline should be carried out in a spirit of gentleness, humility, and patience.

22. (a) In verse 20, Paul expresses his desire that Hymenaeus and Alexander "may learn not to blaspheme." Regarding the excommunication of a man from the congregation at Corinth, Paul expresses the hope that the man will experience "the destruction of the flesh, so that his spirit may be saved in the day of the Lord" (1 Corinthians 5:5). Excommunication, then, is intended to lead the sinner to repentance and faith. (b) Excommunication is also intended to prevent the sinner from leading others into sin. (c) The excommunicated sinner who repents should be welcomed back into full fellowship in the church.

Living the Faith Together

1 Timothy 2–3

Preparing for the Session

Central Focus

1 Timothy 3:14 summarizes this section: "I am writing these things to you so that, if I delay, you may know how one ought to behave in the household of God." First Paul warns Timothy about those who use the truth for their own gain (session 1). Then he outlines the way God's household must order and conduct itself in its response to the Word of truth. The things Paul mentions here—intercessory prayer, the conduct of women, the characteristics of a pastor—flow from the life-giving Word of God. Paul recognizes that these things might not be self-evident to the church and that they might not measure up to human logic because "the mystery of godliness is great" (1 Timothy 3:16 NIV).

Objectives

That the participant, as a child of God and with the Holy Spirit's help, will be led deeper into the divinely given realizations that

1. the church, the body of Christ, has a certain shape and order according to the Gospel of salvation;
2. the individual Christian's place in the church has to do with divinely created love for God and love for neighbor, not personal gain;
3. "the mystery of godliness" (1 Timothy 3:16) requires that each Christian listen to God's truth and hold it, not pass judgment on it or decide whether it personally applies.

For the Small-Group Leader

Small-Group Discussion Helps

In session 1 we considered that God has spoken. He spoke in the old times by the prophets. But in the new order of things it is Christ through whom and in whom God speaks. And that is the best revelation of all. In this week's study we hear the call of God to pay attention to this better, this best, message.

Day 1 • 1 Timothy 2:1–7

1. Answers will vary. Our prayers for local authorities would include police officers, city council members, mayors, and judges. Parents and pastors, teachers and school board members could also be among the authorities for whom we could pray. Foreign leaders as well, including those antagonistic to our own country, should be included in the requests we present to God.

2. (a) Paul's admonition to pray for "all" in authority is made even more striking when we remember that evil individuals can occupy positions of authority over us. They, too, are needful and deserving of our prayers. Romans 13 leads us to see that "[the authorities] that exist have been instituted by God." Tyranny is preferable to chaos. Moreover, God is at work even through evil rulers—for the sake of His church. For that reason we should not only pray for all in authority, but also submit to them and honor them. (b) When civil rulers overstep their proper role of maintaining order and punishing evildoers and order us to disobey God and His Word, we are to obey God rather than the evil authority.

3. (a) God wants all people to be saved. (b) This salvation can only be achieved through the "one mediator between God and men," Jesus the Christ, "who gave Himself as a ransom" for all as He paid for our sin when He died on the cross.

In our world a mediator is one who works between two parties to resolve differences. Jesus is the mediator who offered Himself on the cross to make peace between God and sinners. (c) Answers will vary. Christ as our mediator brings us not only peace with God our Father, but also a new life with God.

Day 2 • 1 Timothy 2:8–15

4. (a) Open hands lifted upward are, first of all, empty hands, reflecting the humility and spiritual poverty of the one who prays. But open hands lifted up are also expectant hands, ready to receive. We expect God to answer our prayer, not because of who we are or what we bring to Him, but simply because of His fatherly divine

goodness and mercy. (b) The folding of the hands is a movement that allows the one praying to focus and concentrate on the prayer offered. The busy tasks of life in which the hands are normally engaged are thus unable to distract the one who prays. Kneeling shows reverence, submission, and honor to the God who is addressed in prayer.

5. Immodest or inappropriate dress in public worship could be distracting for other worshipers. To dress in such a way as to draw attention to oneself is especially out of place in public worship, where the attention of all should be directed toward "things that are above, where Christ is, seated at the right hand of God" (Colossians 3:1).

6. (a) Answers will vary. Many Christians fail to distinguish between the *equality* that all believers enjoy through faith in Jesus Christ (expressed in Galatians 3:28) and the differences between males and females set in place at creation. Others see the pastoral office only as a set of "functions" that a woman could perform as well as a man. The pastoral office, however, is a divine institution, given by God, for the good of His church. His Word concerning the qualifications of those who hold the office is clear and should not be ignored. (b) In verse 13, Paul appeals to the creation to highlight the God-given distinction between man and woman. The man was created first. The woman was created second as "a helper fit for him" (Genesis 2:20). (c) In verse 14, Paul appeals to the fall into sin to show the disastrous results that followed when Adam and Eve stepped out of their God-given roles. Rather than *helping* her husband, Eve took the lead in sinning, and her husband followed. Paul is not here pointing out the woman's weakness, but, rather, her abandonment of her role as "helper." (d) Because Adam allowed this to happen, God held him accountable as the one man through whom sin entered the world (Romans 5:12).

7. Women and men are saved eternally by God's grace through faith in Jesus Christ.

Day 3 • 1 Timothy 3:1–7

8. Pastors who meet the qualifications set forth in these verses would be able to devote themselves fully to preaching and teaching the truth of God's Word. Unqualified pastors, on the other hand, would have to defend themselves against scandalous charges, would fail as teachers of sound doctrine, and would undoubtedly bring disgrace upon the church and the Gospel.

9. Just as shepherds tend the flock by providing nourishment, pastors, too, are called to nourish those under their care with the Word and Sacraments. Just as shepherds must guard the flock from predators, pastors too must watch out for "fierce wolves" who will distort the truth and harm the flock.

10. Answers will vary. The pastor's calling is "noble" not because of the man himself. It is a noble calling, rather, because the man stands in the stead of Christ, bringing the gifts of Christ in Word and Sacrament to those he is called to serve.

11. The Scriptures make clear that pastors must maintain a high standard of conduct because they serve as "examples" and "models" of Christian living.

12. (a) This phrase explicitly forbids a pastor to have more than one wife. Implicitly, however, it also upholds the truth that pastors who desire to marry should be allowed to do so. (b) This phrase also speaks of the pastor as a "husband," that is, a male.

Day 4 • 1 Timothy 3:8–13

13. The church at Jerusalem elected seven men to oversee the daily distribution of food to those in need, especially the widows. The selection of these men allowed the apostles to focus their attention primarily on proclaiming the Word of God. (Although these men are not directly called deacons here, the Greek word used to describe their responsibility of "waiting on" tables is the verb from which the noun *deacon* is derived.)

14. We might call a "double-tongued" person "two-face," or someone who talks out of "both sides" of his mouth. These phrases all describe someone who cannot be trusted. Such a one would not be qualified to serve as a leader in the church. Such a person would lead to factions and fighting among church members.

15. The nature of a deacon's work would make it necessary for him to travel from home to home, either to distribute items to those in need, or perhaps to mediate minor disputes and conflicts. Their wives would perhaps be privy to much of this information. Those wives who were respectable and "not slanderers" would be a great asset to the work of their husbands.

16. Pastors are sinners. They are "unworthy" of the high office to which they have been called. Yet, the Word they preach and the efficacy and power of the Sacraments they serve is not diminished because of their own shortcomings. God works through the means of grace

with such tender love and care that not even the unworthiness of the servants weakens or diminishes His gifts! God not only works *through* pastors to build up His church, but He can also work *despite* pastors to accomplish the same.

Day 5 • 1 Timothy 3:14–16

17. (a) "Household of God" might lead us to think of the church as a family, as those who have been made brothers and sisters with one another, as well as brothers and sisters of the Lord Jesus Christ. (b) The "church of the living God" accentuates that the church belongs to God. It brings to mind the promise of Jesus "I will build My church, and the gates of hell shall not prevail against it" (Matthew 16:18). (c) Paul also describes the church as "a pillar and buttress of truth." The pillar and buttress are those parts of a structure that support the entire building. The church is called to uphold and proclaim the truth of the Gospel and to praise the One who calls Himself the way, *the truth,* and the life (John 14:6).

18. As a true man, Jesus took on our human flesh (John 1:14). We call this the incarnation. He shared fully in our humanity so that He might destroy the devil and free us from the fear of death (Hebrews 2:14–15).

19. Jesus was vindicated and justified when the Spirit raised Him from the dead. Our Lord's resurrection is the proof that He is indeed the Son of God and that His doctrine is the truth.

20. Our Lord was "seen by angels" both at His resurrection and at His ascension.

The Truths of the Faith Must Remain Central

1 Timothy 4:1–6:2

Preparing for the Session

Central Focus

A "good servant of Christ Jesus" (4:6) must rebuke those who teach and believe falsely. He must also care for the congregation, especially widows and older men. He must allow no one to abuse (1) the congregation (as might the young widows who want to be placed on the shut-in list without cause), or (2) the good graces of the Christian brother (such as the slave who has a believing master might be tempted). In so doing, the pastor must neither lord his position over the congregation nor allow anyone to look down on him because of the lowliness of his person. His exemplary life will help create the respect that the divinely given pastoral office deserves.

Objectives

That the participant, as a child of God and with the Holy Spirit's help, will be led deeper into the divinely given realizations that

1. the "truths of the faith," drawn from the Scriptures, must remain central in the life of every congregation;
2. the individual Christian's place in the church has to do with the humility that flows from divinely created love for God and love for neighbor, not personal gain (as we also saw in session 2);
3. pastor and congregation alike must view the pastoral office with love and respect, given by God for the care of God's people, not for the exaltation of one person or group over another.

For the Small-Group Leader

Small-Group Discussion Helps

Day 1 • 1 Timothy 4:1–8

1. The "later times" of which Paul writes can best be understood as the entire period between Jesus' earthly ministry and His second coming. The author of Hebrews depicts the "last days" as the days in which God "has spoken to us by His Son" (Hebrews 1:2). Many of the false teachings that Paul ascribes to later times were clearly already present even as he wrote to Timothy.

2. (a) A conscience that has been "seared" is a conscience that has been burned, cauterized. A conscience so traumatized would be numbed and insensible to the difference between right and wrong. It would be unable to distinguish between good and evil. (b) These legalistic false teachers were forbidding people to marry and were forcing them to abstain from certain foods. They failed to recognize that marriage and food are gifts from God, intended for our benefit.

3. (a) Such gifts ought to be received with thanksgiving. (b) It is easy to forget who gives daily bread. If daily bread comes to us only as a result of our work and effort, then there is no reason to receive it with thanksgiving. But asking God for daily bread, as we do in the Lord's Prayer, leads us to view God as the giver. As we receive His good gifts in faith, we are led to respond with thanks and praise.

4. Answers will vary. Regularly hearing the Word, studying the Word, receiving the Lord's Supper, and attending public worship are among the "exercises" which build up the faith of every Christian. The Spirit-wrought result is godliness and holy living.

Day 2 • 1 Timothy 4:9–16

5. (a) Jesus is the Savior of *all people* in that His perfect life and atoning death on the cross were offered for the sins of all people. "In Christ God was reconciling *the world* to Himself," Paul writes in 2 Corinthians 5:19. Out of love for "the world," God gave His one and only Son. Whether people believe in Christ or not, it remains objectively true that Christ died for all. (b) Not all people will be saved, however, since many ignore the Savior's invitation and reject the Holy Spirit.

6. The truths of the faith must continually be taught to every generation. Jesus Himself gave the mandate to make disciples of nations, baptizing them and "teaching them to observe all that I have commanded you" (Matthew 28:20). When God's Word is no longer taught, some Christians will be deceived into false belief and despair, some will abandon the faith, and the Holy Spirit will have little opportunity to convert unbelievers to faith in Christ.

7. Answers will vary. While all of God's Word is inspired and useful, the Scripture readings chosen for use in public worship should be especially edifying and instructive. They should be helpful and relevant to the child of God as his or her faith in Christ finds expression in vocation and daily life.

8. Holy living can only be shaped and directed by doctrine that is pure and correct. The "myths and endless genealogies" that the false teachers were promoting (1:4) could do nothing to cause an increase in holy living. "Without faith," the author of Hebrews writes, "it is impossible to please [God]" (11:6). Conversely, a life filled with wickedness cannot properly bear witness to the truth of God's revelation in Christ. As Jesus said, "A healthy tree cannot bear bad fruit, nor can a diseased tree bear good fruit" (Matthew 7:18). A Christian should, therefore, be leery of one who purports to proclaim the truth but lives an outwardly evil life.

Day 3 • 1 Timothy 5:1–10

9. Older men are to be treated as fathers, younger men as brothers, older women as mothers, and younger women as sisters. Christians are to relate to one another as members of the same family.

10. (a) In an age when husbands were the chief providers and defenders, becoming a widow was a frightening prospect. In addition to the unlikelihood of finding employment, there would have been no Medicare or Social Security income, no life insurance benefit, and no pension plan from which to draw an income. (b) Some widows, however, were better off than others. Some were "truly widows." Others, perhaps, had enough savings or resources to live comfortably. In providing assistance to widows, the church was to take such differences into consideration.

11. (a) Paul describes the care that the aged receive from their children and grandchildren as a "return." The children had *received* care—and thus it is appropriate that they make some return. (b) Paul writes that care offered in such a way is "pleasing in the sight of God." (c) Answers will vary. Too often, perhaps, the elderly are seen as "problems" and not as "people." We sinfully gauge a person's worth in terms of their productivity, instead of seeing every human life as a gift from God. (The small-group leader will want to exercise care with this topic not to increase the guilt of participants who may have close family members living in nursing homes or other care facilities. Such arrangements for care should not be disparaged and often are the best option for maintaining the health and dignity of older persons.)

Day 4 • 1 Timothy 5:11–16

12. To be eligible for support from the church, a widow had to be over sixty years old. She had to have lived a life of faithfulness to her husband. She also had to be known for her good works and hospitality.

13. Sins of the tongue seem innocent and minor. But as St. James points out, the tongue can be "a world of unrighteousness" (3:6). Just as a small, insignificant spark can ignite an entire forest, so also can our gossip and slander do great harm to reputations and relationships within the body of Christ.

14. Answers will vary. The one who gossips and slanders hopes to make himself look good by tearing others down. By sharing "juicy" information, he sets himself up as one who has power and knowledge that others don't. In short, gossip is perfectly suited to satisfy our sinful pride and desire for power.

15. Do not ask participants to share their answers to the questions.

Day 5 • 1 Timothy 5:17–6:2

16. The text indicates that "explains God's Word effectively" is number 1; good administrator is 2. Answers may vary regarding the other listed characteristics. While some might contend that a pastor should lovingly accept all viewpoints, this runs counter to the very theme of the Epistle we are studying, in which Timothy is specifically instructed to silence the viewpoints of those who are teaching falsely.

17. These passages are quoted to show that pastors should be paid for their work of preaching and teaching.

18. Two or three witnesses must be willing to testify before Timothy should entertain any accusation against an elder.

19. Rebuking a sinning pastor in the presence of other pastors could have at least two benefits. It could, first of all, serve as a warning to other pastors not to fall into the same sin. Secondly, it could afford the sinning pastor the opportunity to express his repentance openly, and then to receive absolution and the support of his brothers in the ministry.

20. (a) Paul urges those believers under the yoke of slavery to respect their masters. This should be done, he writes, "so that the name of God and the teaching may not be reviled." Also, the slave is helping a fellow believer. (b) Allow volunteers to share their responses.

The Value of Faith above All Other Things

1 Timothy 6:3–21

Preparing for the Session

Central Focus

After outlining the way in which the pastor interacts with and cares for the members of his congregation (session 3), Paul now returns to the beginning of his Letter to Timothy, speaking the same sort of exhortation to faithfulness as he did in chapter 1 (session 1). Paul never allows himself or the church to stray too far from sound doctrine (that is, teaching)! In this summary section of his Letter, he calls upon his friend Timothy to focus again on the teaching he has received, to resist the temptations of wealth and to "pursue righteousness, godliness, faith, love, steadfastness, gentleness" (1 Timothy 6:11). Such labors, made possible by the Holy Spirit through His divine Word, will result in eternal treasures!

Objectives

That the participant, as a child of God and with the Holy Spirit's help, will be led deeper into the divinely given realizations that

1. the objectives, goals, and commitments of the world spell destruction for the Christian faith;
2. "the good confession" (1 Timothy 6:13) and strong doctrine are worth more than money, goods, family, friends, or anything else in the world;
3. God's people, no matter how they might struggle financially or otherwise, never are forgotten by God. He sees them, cares for them, and has established an eternal home for them in His presence.

For the Small-Group Leader

Small-Group Discussion Helps

Day 1 • 1 Timothy 6:3–5

1. Answers will vary. (a) Just as a healthy diet and lifestyle can increase our physical strength and stamina, the "sound words" of Jesus Christ strengthen our faith as they bring the forgiveness of sins. As the promises of God are applied to our weakness, He blesses us with His strength to bear our crosses. The benefits and joys of these "healthy words" are not only felt in this present life, but will also ultimately lead us by faith to "the life of the world to come." (b) False doctrine is "unhealthy" because it does not come from God. It serves to weaken our faith, to manufacture doubt concerning God's promises, and to lead us down pathways that are spiritually harmful. Taken to its devilish extreme, false doctrine could lead us to reject the faith and lose the gift of eternal life.

2. In Matthew 7:24–27, Jesus describes His words as a "rock" on which those who are wise can build securely. In John 12:48, Jesus tells of the judgment and condemnation that await those who reject His words. In John chapter 17, in His High Priestly Prayer, Jesus reveals that He has given His disciples the Word of the Father. This Word is, in its very essence, truth.

3. (a) Such a one is "puffed up with conceit and understands nothing. He has an unhealthy craving for controversy and for quarrels about words." (b) The effects of such false teaching include "envy, dissension, slander, evil suspicions, and constant friction." (c) Check everything on the basis of Scripture.

4. Those who do not agree to "the sound words of our Lord Jesus Christ" and those who "create obstacles contrary to the doctrine that you have been taught" (Romans 16:17) must shoulder the blame for discord and division in the church. It is the deliberate teaching of error, not truth, that results in strife and malicious words within the church.

Day 2 • 1 Timothy 6:6–10

5. (a) Answers will vary. To be content is to be satisfied and happy with what you have. (b) Answers will vary. Contentment does not come naturally to most people. Our Old Adam is never satisfied. He always leads us to look longingly at the "greener" pastures on the "other side" of the fence. Contentment is made especially difficult to achieve by the constant bombardment of advertising that flows into our lives. Most advertising is designed to make us think that what we have isn't good

enough and that we can only be happy if we acquire the advertised product.

6. In Philippians chapter 4, Paul writes of having learned the "secret" of contentment: "I can do all things through [Christ] who strengthens me" (4:13). In other words, the Lord Jesus is the true giver of contentment in the life of the Christian. The author of Hebrews, likewise, recognizes that contentment flows from the God who has promised never to leave us and never to forsake us.

7. It would seem that Christians can indeed set their sights on better things, and do so without sinning. However, blessings that are currently enjoyed, as well as future blessings not yet received, must always be regarded "with thanksgiving" (4:4). That is to say, we must understand that what we now have is a wonderful gift from God. Likewise, the "better things" we may one day have must also be viewed as wonderful gifts from God. But if our striving for "better things" leads us to be ungrateful for what we already have, then God's gift of contentment has been lost.

8. Contentment is a good gift from God. It enables us to do all things "in the name of the Lord Jesus, giving thanks to God the Father" (Colossians 3:17). It empowers us to "[render] service with a good will" (Ephesians 6:7) in the callings God has given us. Complacency, however, implies that tasks are done only halfheartedly and without any thankfulness. God has not called us to lives of complacency, but contentment.

9. The love of money is a tool for temptation. It is a "snare" that leads to "ruin and destruction." As the root of all evil, it can entice people to wander from the faith and to be pierced with many griefs.

Day 3 • 1 Timothy 6:11–16

10. (a) Answers will vary widely. Many people flee from responsibility and authority and hard work. We flee from the commands God has given us. We flee from bodily danger and harm. We flee from boredom and conflict. (b) The "things" from which Timothy is to flee probably include the love of money, which is mentioned in verse 10.

11. Even as we flee from the love of money, we should pursue righteousness, godliness, faith, love, endurance, and gentleness.

12. In Ephesians 6:13–17, Paul describes "the whole armor of God." Fighting "the good fight" means being girded with "the belt of truth." "The breastplate of righteousness" offers great protection. "The shield of faith" allows the Christian to "extinguish all the flaming darts of the evil one." "The helmet of salvation" and "the sword of the Spirit" complete the attire for fighting "the good fight of the faith."

13. Jesus has promised to be present "where two or three are gathered" in His name (Matthew 18:20). When Christians come together for the Divine Service they can hear and recognize the Lord as His Word is proclaimed and preached. Through the miracle of Holy Baptism (Romans 6) we are united with Jesus in His death and resurrection. In the Lord's Supper (1 Corinthians 11) Jesus gives His very body and blood for us sinners to eat and drink. By His own promise we can know with confidence that our gracious Lord is at work in our lives through these precious means.

Day 4 • 1 Timothy 6:17–19

14. (a) They should not be arrogant. (b) They should place their hope in God and not in wealth. (c) They should be rich in good deeds, generous and willing to share.

15. (a) God desires that people turn from their idols and acknowledge Him as the Giver—their Creator. (b) Idolatry—worshiping things rather than the God who made all things. Along with this come all manner of evil thoughts and deeds. (c) Answers will vary. Most people do not believe that all they have comes from God. Instead, the most prevalent attitude concerning possessions could be summarized in this way: "I worked for it. I earned it. It's mine!" Only through faith in Jesus Christ is the believer able to see that God Himself provides us with all that we need for this life.

16. It is not a sin to be rich or to have plenty. It was God, after all, who caused the rich man's ground to produce such a bumper crop. Nor was it necessarily sinful for the man to build bigger barns to hold the harvest. Even his plan to "take life easy" could be interpreted as a desire to enjoy God's gifts. But God called him a "fool" (Luke 12:20). Jesus notes that he was "not rich toward God" (v. 21). To be rich toward God is *to believe* that He is the giver of all good things. The rich man's sin was that he did not believe this. This can be seen in the man's use of personal pronouns in verses 17–18 ("my crops," "my barns," "my grain," "my goods"). The crops, the barns, and the goods were all gifts from God, yet the rich man regarded them as his alone. Because he viewed everything as *his alone*, the rich man shows no inclination to

share his goods with his neighbor (another sin). Such sharing would have come naturally if he had viewed his riches as a gift from God.

Day 5 • 1 Timothy 6:20–21

17. In 1:11, the "deposit" is described as "the glorious gospel of the blessed God." In 1:15, this Gospel is succinctly expressed in the saying, "Christ Jesus came into the world to save sinners." The deposit is expressed through a hymn about Jesus in 3:16. In 4:10, the "deposit" is seen through the "living God, who is the Savior of all people."

18. (a) In verse 20, Timothy is told to "avoid" the purveyors of godless chatter and pseudo-knowledge. (b) Paul's concern is that these false doctrines could cause some under Timothy's spiritual care to wander from the faith—to lose the gift of their salvation. For the believer to have "an open mind" in the face of such spiritual danger is risky and foolish.

19. Ask for volunteers to share their answers with the group.

Faith in the Midst of Hardship

2 Timothy 1:1–2:13

Preparing for the Session

Central Focus

Paul wrote this Letter while imprisoned in Rome (2 Timothy 1:16–17). Feeling lonely and abandoned, the apostle greatly desired to see his beloved Timothy again (2 Timothy 1:4), but he had also begun to think that he would likely die for the faith before such a visit could be made. Thus, while Paul cherished his warm memory of Timothy's "sincere faith" (2 Timothy 1:5), he wrote his friend a last will and testament, outlining the most important things that he wants Timothy to know and to believe. He calls upon Timothy to persevere in teaching the Gospel in a pure and unchanged form, even if such teaching should result in hardships endured for the faith (2 Timothy 2:3).

Objectives

That the participant, as a child of God and with the Holy Spirit's help, will be led deeper into the divinely given realizations that

1. Paul in his inspired Letter calls all Christians to faithfulness to the pure Gospel, no matter what hardships they may endure as a result;
2. Christ saved us and called us to a holy life because of His own purpose and grace, and not because of any good thing we could say or do;
3. the Gospel of our Lord Jesus Christ gives both courage and faith to God's people, with the result that they may face their hardships and struggles without fear but in the confidence that God will surely fulfill all His promises in Christ Jesus.

For the Small-Group Leader

Small-Group Discussion Helps

Day 1 • 2 Timothy 1:1–4

1. Answers will vary. Under these circumstances one would expect the tone of the Epistle to be solemn, straightforward, and affectionate. In terms of content, Paul might be expected to articulate those doctrines and exhortations that are of greatest importance. Other matters of lesser importance might not be addressed.

2. (a) In the first sentence, Paul accentuates the "promise of the life" that is in Christ Jesus. (b) Paul is referring to the life that God gives through faith in Jesus Christ. He has brought "life and immortality to light through the gospel" (2:10), and promises eternal life to all who believe (John 3:16).

3. Answers will vary. On the one hand, thanksgiving often does not come easily in the midst of trials and suffering. Other feelings, such as anger, sadness, and worry can sometimes crowd out thoughts of thankfulness. On the other hand, suffering can also sharpen our spiritual vision, allowing us to see the many blessings in our lives with greater clarity, prompting expressions of thanks to God. Thankfulness is not dependent upon earthly circumstances or possessions. Whether living in plenty or in want (Philippians 4:12), and even under extreme weakness (2 Corinthians 12:7–10), we cannot be robbed of the treasure of our salvation. Nothing can separate us from the love of God in Christ Jesus. This Good News can create thankful hearts in us, even when earthly circumstances are dire.

4. (a) Answers will vary. A clear conscience could be described as a mind at peace in the forgiveness of Jesus Christ. Neither personal guilt over past sins nor the accusations of Satan have any power over the child of God who enjoys a clear conscience. (b) Earlier in his life Paul (Saul) had been an enemy of Christ and His church. With great zeal he had persecuted the church of God and tried to destroy it (Galatians 1:13). He hunted down and imprisoned those with faith in Jesus (Acts 8:1–3). (c) Both Psalm 32 and James 5:16 speak of God's gift of confession. Attempts to hide our sins are

futile and harmful. God invites us to confess them, with the assurance that He will forgive us and cleanse our guilty consciences.

Day 2 • 2 Timothy 1:5–12

5. (a) The role of parents in shaping the faith of their children cannot be overstated. Parents have the sacred duty to bring up their children "in the discipline and instruction of the Lord" (Ephesians 6:4). At all times and places parents are to impress the Word of God on their children (Deuteronomy 6:4–9). (b) Faithful and prayerful instruction and modeling of the Christian faith can, by the power of God's Holy Spirit, result in faith in children and grandchildren.

6. Timothy's special gift likely included his ability to serve as a minister of Jesus Christ (1 Timothy 4:6) as well as the teaching that accompanied that calling (1 Timothy 4:11–14). Paul undoubtedly believed that Timothy was especially gifted at directing the affairs of the church (1 Timothy 5:17), which is evidenced by the great responsibilities Paul had entrusted to him at Ephesus.

7. Timothy's personality was perhaps somewhat timid at times.

8. Our salvation was accomplished by God in Christ. It was accomplished by God's own purpose and grace, not because of anything we have done. It was wondrously planned before the beginning of time.

9. As time permits, allow volunteers to share their summaries.

Day 3 • 2 Timothy 1:13–18

10. Paul clearly believed that his words were to be kept and followed in their entirety. What he passed along in his Epistles were the very words and commands of God. He would undoubtedly have only the sharpest condemnation for those who would seek to divide the words of his Epistles as either "God's Word" or "Paul's word."

11. Answers will vary somewhat. At its heart, however, this good "deposit" is the very Gospel itself—the Good News of the salvation God has accomplished for us in Christ.

12. (a) The Holy Spirit helps us to guard the good deposit as He teaches us and enables us to call to mind the Word of God. (b) In Ephesians 5:18–20, Paul writes of being "filled with the Spirit." To be filled by the Holy Spirit is to be under the Spirit's control as He leads us in worship, service, and witness. (c) The Holy Spirit helps us in our weakness as He intercedes (prays) for the saints.

13. (a) Paul was not preaching to a packed, growing congregation; rather, he was languishing in a cold dungeon. Many of his co-workers had apparently deserted him. False teachers were working hard to corrupt sound doctrine in the congregations Paul had planted. A modern pastor, presenting a similar record of achievement, would be scoffed at by many. However, the point can be made that he held to his convictions despite persecution and was indeed successful because of that. This very good question can be discussed from two perspectives. (b) A pastor's ministry should be evaluated not on the basis of results (only God produces those), but on the basis of faithfulness to his calling. Many dimensions of that calling are set forth in the Pastoral Epistles. These include preaching, correcting, rebuking, encouraging, and instructing with great patience.

Day 4 • 2 Timothy 2:1–7

14. (a) Answers will vary. Grace is the unmerited, undeserved love of God that comes through Jesus Christ. It is by this grace that we are saved from sin and death. This grace is all-sufficient, sustaining us even in the face of weakness and hardship. (b) Invite volunteers to share how they have been strengthened by the grace of Jesus.

15. (a) The comparison to a soldier would highlight the hardships and dangers Timothy would face as a minister. A soldier is not distracted by other affairs but is focused on pleasing his commanding officer. Timothy, similarly, would have to be focused on following Paul's directives for the congregations at Ephesus. (b) As an athlete must compete according to the rules, Timothy must carry out his ministry with a purity of life and doctrine. Endurance and perseverance are other athletic qualities Timothy will find useful in his ministry. (c) As with a farmer, Timothy will patiently plant the seed of God's Word and patiently wait for God to give the growth. Such effort will be rewarded at the time of harvest.

16. (a) "A mind is a terrible thing to waste," especially where God's Word is concerned! God desires that we "read, mark, learn and inwardly digest" His Word. Family devotions, public worship, and Bible studies such as *LifeLight* are all valuable opportunities for applying our minds to the Holy Scriptures. (b) This is a wonderful promise for those who apply their minds to God's

Word. "He *will* give you insight." There are no ifs, ands, or buts here. God will reward you with insight as you hear and reflect on His Word. Your study of the Bible is not in vain.

Day 5 • 2 Timothy 2:8–13

17. Strive to help the participants understand the following truths: (a) Psalm 49:7–8—A mere man could not meet the demands of divine holiness and justice. Only God could reconcile the world to Himself (2 Corinthians 5:19) and keep the Law perfectly for us. It was *God's* blood that was shed for us (Acts 20:28). (b) It was necessary for Jesus to be true man to obey (fulfill) the Law as the substitute for all people (Romans 5:19) and to be able to suffer and die for our sin (Hebrews 2:14).

18. (a) Answers will vary but may include some of the following: "He was a champion for the rights of the poor and downtrodden." "He was a revolutionary." "He is an example for us to follow." "He was an extremely religious man." While there may be elements of truth in these and other descriptions of Jesus, they all fall short of confessing Him as the divine-human Son of God and the Savior from sin and death. (b) They are literally a matter of life or death. Refusing to trust in the Christ of Scripture leads to eternal death apart from Him.

19. (a) By means of our Baptism we have died with Christ and been raised to new life in Him. The phrase of verse 11, "If we have died [past tense] with Him, we will also live with Him," alludes to our Baptism. Through Baptism, we enter into a vital faith relationship with Christ. It is a means of receiving God's grace, and it depicts graphically what happens as a result of our union with Christ. (b) The phrase of verse 12, "If we endure, we will also reign with Him," would have specific application to the endurance of persecution and martyrdom that Paul and others were facing. There would be great comfort in knowing that "the sufferings of this present time are not worth comparing with the glory" that awaits those who live under the cross in this life (Romans 8:18).

20. Answers will vary. As time permits, encourage participants to share their responses.

Faith Put to Action in Life

2 Timothy 2:14–3:17

Preparing for the Session

Central Focus

Believing he is near death, Paul wrote this Letter to Timothy as a theological last will and testament, stressing to his younger friend the great need to remain faithful to "the pattern of the sound words" (2 Timothy 1:13) and the "good deposit" (1:14) that had been entrusted to him. Part of Timothy's faithfulness will require that he entrust others with the pastoral office. In his First Letter to Timothy, Paul outlined the qualifications for those who would become pastors (1 Timothy 3:1–7). Now, as he thinks about Timothy's work of entrusting others, Paul contemplates the sort of temptations and struggles these men will face as they undertake their labors.

Objectives

That the participant, as a child of God and with the Holy Spirit's help, will be led deeper into the divinely given realizations that

1. the Word of God, rather than "irreverent babble" (2:16), must remain at the center of the church's life and conversation;
2. those who wish to live piously according to the Word of God will be persecuted (2:12), even by people in the church who have "the appearance of godliness, but [deny] its power" (3:5);
3. the living Word of the Scriptures is not merely information, but it is the very power of God that actively guards and protects you against harm and danger.

For the Small-Group Leader

Small-Group Discussion Helps

Day 1 • 2 Timothy 2:14–19

1. This Epistle was Paul's final Epistle. As he wrote it he was in prison, apparently in chains. He was all alone except for Luke. The end of his earthly life seemed to be drawing near.

2. (a) The Gospel—the Good News of what God has done for us in the gift of His Son—giving us forgiveness of sin and eternal life. (b) Faithful preachers "rightly [handle] the word of truth," the Gospel. Teachers of false doctrine want to have their own and their hearers' ears "itched" to satisfy their own evil inclinations.

3. As time permits, allow volunteers to share and discuss their responses. Cancer usually begins as something small and insignificant. In its earliest stages it is often unable to be detected. In the same way, false doctrine in the church often begins as just a "new idea" with a small number of adherents. It hardly seems threatening at the outset. But just as cancer grows and spreads when left untreated, so too does false doctrine grow and gain acceptance when it is unaddressed by pastors and teachers and laypersons in the church. Furthermore, a cancer that is advanced will often respond to only the most drastic treatments. Radical surgery is sometimes necessary. In the same way, the church must often take drastic measures of church discipline to confront and correct those who are actively promoting error. Finally, just as cancer is sometimes a deadly disease, false doctrine can destroy faith and thereby cause its adherents to lose the gift of eternal life.

4. (a) In 1 Corinthians 15, Paul makes it clear that our hope in Christ is not for this life only. In fact, he writes that those who do not believe in the resurrection of the dead "are of all people most to be pitied" (v. 19). Christ's resurrection is the "firstfruits" (v. 23) of those who have died in faith. His resurrection is the guarantee that our bodies will also be raised from death. (b) Hymenaeus and Philetus were teaching that the resurrection had already taken place. By this false teaching they had destroyed the faith of some.

Day 2 • 2 Timothy 2:20–26

5. (a) In John 8:31–32, Jesus tells us that the truth is knowable. The truth is found in His teaching and it brings freedom to those who hold to His teaching. (b) In John 15:5, Jesus describes the relationship between Himself and His followers as that of a vine and its branches. It is as we remain in Him that we are able to bear much fruit. (c) In Romans 16:17–18, Paul warns us to "watch out for" and "avoid" those who bring division

by their false teaching. (d) In 1 John 4:1, the apostle tells us to "test the spirits." In other words, Christians are to evaluate and judge everything based on the Word of God so as to identify and stay clear of false prophets.

6. (a) When a spirit of gentleness prevails in the home, it allows the home to be a place of comfort and security. When family members deal gently with one another, it fosters trust and intimacy. Best of all, gentleness creates a home environment that is conducive to a family devotional life centered in God's Word, prayer, and praise. (b) Gentleness in the congregation is edifying. It builds up God's people and creates an environment that is nurturing and inviting. In contrast, harsh and critical words tear down and sap the energy of God's servants. (c) Gentleness should also characterize our evangelism efforts. Confrontation and fighting is attractive to no one, especially to unbelievers. A person cannot be argued and harangued into believing. But a spirit of gentleness can foster an open dialogue through which God's Word and Spirit can be heard and received.

Day 3 • 2 Timothy 3:1–9

7. With his use of the phrase "last days," Paul is referring to the entire period of time between Christ's first coming and His return on the Last Day.

8. Answers will vary.

9. (a) There are a multitude of such organizations, but some of the more well-known groups would include Mormons, Jehovah's Witnesses, the Masons and other lodges, Christian Scientists, and the like. (b) In verse 5, we are told to "avoid such people." (c) We are called to witness to our faith by showing love and sharing Jesus with people even as we avoid joining in ungodly behavior (Matthew 5:9–11). We need to avoid association with those who claim to be Christian but live blatantly unrepentant lives.

10. (a) In Matthew 16, Jesus calls the church His own and promises that not even the gates of hades will prevail against it. (b) In John 16, Jesus acknowledges the trouble that His followers will face in this world. But He also adds that He has "overcome the world" (v. 33). He now shares that victory with all who believe. (c) In 2 Timothy 3:9, we can take comfort in the fact that such godlessness has limits. The folly of those who oppose God's truth will eventually become apparent.

Day 4 • 2 Timothy 3:10–13

11. (a) Although all the items listed by Paul in these verses are important and beneficial, his teaching is the basis for all that follows. It is by means of what Paul has taught that men and women (like Timothy) came to faith in Jesus Christ and were saved. It was his teaching (really, the Gospel itself) that, in turn, shaped and directed Paul's way of life, purpose, and so on. (b) What Paul describes as "my teaching" is not "his" because it originated with him. It is "his" in the sense that his very life and identity had centered around it. He did not teach his own words, but his teaching was actually the very Word of God.

12. Paul expresses his "aim" in a number of ways in Philippians 3. His purpose is "knowing Christ Jesus," being "found in Him," having the "righteousness from God that depends on faith," sharing "His sufferings," and to "attain the resurrection from the dead."

13. (a) At Antioch Paul and Barnabas were expelled from the city. (b) At Iconium there was a plot to mistreat and stone them from which they fled. (c) At Lystra Paul was stoned and left for dead.

Day 5 • 2 Timothy 3:14–17

14. (a) From the way this word is used in Holy Scripture, it would seem that it is never too early to start teaching little ones the truths of God's Word. (b) God's Word makes no distinction between children who are born and children who are still in their mothers' wombs. The living but unborn are, therefore, persons in the sight of God from the time of conception. As such, they live under the protection of God's command not to hurt or harm our neighbor, but to help and support him or her in every physical need.

15. (a) God the Holy Spirit gave His chosen writers both the thoughts they expressed and the very words that they wrote. The Bible is, therefore, without error. (b) Participants should disagree with the statement because of the word contains. As the statement reads, it could imply that only "parts" or "sections" of the Bible are really God's Word. It further implies that these "parts" are merely "contained" within the Bible, which is a collection of God's Word and man's word. A more precise statement would be "The Bible is the Word of God."

16. It is Satan who seeks to deceive us and cause us to doubt the authenticity of God's Word. His perennial question is constantly whispered into the ears of every child of God, "Did God really say?"

17. Emphasize the clear promise given here that God's Word makes us thoroughly equipped for every good work. As time permits, encourage participants to share their remembrance of the Word in their lives.

Guard against Those Things That Attack Faith

2 Timothy 4; Titus 1

Preparing for the Session

Central Focus

In the last chapter of 2 Timothy, Paul summarizes the most important things he wants Timothy to remember and to do. His message to Titus (probably written between the two Letters to Timothy) is essentially the same as his message to Timothy: the pastor must serve faithfully! Thus we will see that the life of the Christian faith, lived by pastor and by laypeople alike, remains basically the same no matter where or when it is lived. Even today, sin still afflicts God's people; false teachers still spread their lies; Jesus' blood still gives forgiveness and life; God's Word and Spirit still preserve and protect those whom He has called to be His own.

Objectives

That the participant, as a child of God and with the Holy Spirit's help, will be led deeper into the divinely given realizations that

1. God's Word will faithfully guard and sustain all God's saints in their time of need, as it did for Paul in what he believed were the waning days of his life;
2. even if friends and family should abandon God's saints, the abiding presence of the Holy Spirit in the Word shall remain (which is part of the reason why faithfulness to the Word is so essential);
3. that God calls all pastors and all Christians to the same sort of faithfulness to which He calls Timothy and Titus.

For the Small-Group Leader

Small-Group Discussion Helps

Day 1 • 2 Timothy 4:1–8

1. All of Paul's preaching and all of Timothy's preaching was proclaimed in view of the fact that Jesus Christ will one day come again to judge the living and the dead. It is only through the preaching of the Word that men and women can rightly be prepared to face that day. If indeed "faith comes from hearing" (Romans 10:17), then the preaching task of Timothy and all other preachers is given an urgency and importance that can be attributed to no other spoken words. The preaching of the Word creates and sustains the faith by which believers are reckoned as righteous for Jesus' sake. Preaching, therefore, is a matter of life and death.

2. (a) Jesus' first "appearing" was when He came to earth as true man and true God. The purpose of His appearing in human flesh was to save us, and to destroy death and bring "life and immortality to light through the gospel" (2 Timothy 1:9–10). (b) The purpose of His second coming will be to judge the living and the dead. In Palestine sheep and goats were regularly pastured together. But at night they were divided into separate folds. Here Jesus, the Good Shepherd, separates His "sheep"—His believers who trusted in Him for salvation—from those who rejected Him.

3. (a) In Acts 20:27, Paul recounts how his preaching had included "the whole counsel of God." The preacher cannot disregard or "dance around" sections of God's Word that his hearers may find distasteful. This does not mean that he must preach sermons covering every chapter and verse of the Bible. It does mean that the message of salvation must be announced in its completeness (i.e., Law *and* Gospel). (b) Revelation 22:18–19 contains a warning against adding to or taking away from God's Word. Preachers, too, must be careful to handle God's Word properly, not adding their own personal opinions to what God has clearly revealed in His Word. (c) In John 5:39, Jesus makes clear that the Holy Scriptures testify about Him. Jesus Christ is the key to the correct proclamation of God's Word. For this reason, good

preaching will always have at its center the death and resurrection of Jesus.

4. Even as God's Old Testament people worshiped Him through sacrificial offerings, so Paul gives up His life as an offering to Christ—a joyful departure to be with Christ!

5. (a) Through faith in Jesus Christ, Paul possessed the perfect righteousness of Jesus. Jesus' perfect record of obedience counted for Paul. (b) Just as Paul was perfectly righteous, he was simultaneously a sinner. His own sinful nature was constantly "waging war" (Romans 7:23) against the holy desires and actions prompted by his "new man" (Ephesians 2:15). (c) It is only when we leave this earthly life and receive the crown of righteousness that we are rescued from all temptation and sin. The new heaven and new earth will be the home of righteousness (2 Peter 3:13). Sin and its wages will be gone forever.

Day 2 • 2 Timothy 4:9–22

6. With the end of his life quickly approaching, Paul likely desired the comfort, courage, and peace God gives through His Word.

7. The rescue of which Paul is so confident is likely a spiritual rescue and not a physical deliverance from his earthly chains. This is the same kind of rescue for which every Christian prays with the words "Deliver us from evil." As Luther explains in the Small Catechism, "We pray in this petition . . . that our Father in heaven would rescue us from every evil of body and soul, possessions and reputation, and finally, when our last hour comes, give us a blessed end, and graciously take us from this valley of sorrow to Himself in heaven."

8. Regarding Alexander, Paul writes, "The Lord will repay him according to his deeds" (v. 14). In Romans 12, we are reminded that revenge (repayment of evil) falls under God's jurisdiction and not our own. Our concern is to live in peace with everyone and to "overcome evil with good" (Romans 12:21).

9. Answers will vary. Invite those who are comfortable doing so to share their answers.

Day 3 • Titus 1:1–4

10. (a) Galatians 2:1–5. In this passage we learn that Titus accompanied Paul and Barnabas to Jerusalem. Furthermore, we learn that Titus was an uncircumcised Greek. (b) 2 Corinthians 7:5–7. Here Paul recounts the comfort he received from Titus when they were united in Macedonia. At that meeting Titus also brought word to Paul from the church at Corinth. (c) 2 Timothy 4:10. Paul briefly mentions here that Titus had been sent to Dalmatia.

11. What a wonderful listing! We have received mercy and are made "a royal priesthood" (1 Peter 2:9)—free to live eternally for Him who died for us!

12. Those who received and heard the apostles received and heard Jesus Himself. Jesus gave the apostles the authority to speak and preach on His behalf.

13. (a) Knowledge alone does not save. Knowledge can simply be "head" knowledge—intellectual assent that even the devils have. They know and believe what the Scriptures say, but they have no faith. Knowledge is the content of the faith—the doctrines and teachings Timothy and Titus were called to proclaim. (b) While faith is based on knowledge and conviction, it is never a bare intellectual knowledge but is an attitude of the heart. It is *trust* in what God has done for us in Christ—giving us forgiveness of sin and life eternal.

14. Answers will vary but should reflect the following traits of God's elect: They are "exiles" (Hebrews 11:3) in the world whose true home is in heaven. They have been chosen by God, according to the foreknowledge of the Father. They are sanctified (made holy) by the Spirit, resulting in obedience and the cleansing that comes from the blood of Jesus Christ.

15. In Ephesians 4, Paul writes of the "one Lord, one faith, one baptism" that all Christians share. In Acts 2:42, we read of the first Christians, who devoted themselves to the apostles' doctrine, the breaking of bread (Holy Communion), and prayer.

Day 4 • Titus 1:5–9

16. (a) In his Epistle to Titus, Paul says absolutely nothing that would forbid someone who is a recent convert from serving as an elder. (b) This difference in qualifications could mean that the church at Crete was much younger than the congregations around Ephesus. Perhaps the vast majority of Christians at Crete were *all* recent converts. Under these special circumstances, an otherwise qualified man could be considered for service as an elder.

17. (a) Answers will vary. Some might view such rebuking negatively because someone they love is affiliated

with such a group. Others might view such refuting as a personal attack. Such rebuking certainly goes against the popular modern notion that "it doesn't matter what you believe, as long as you're sincere in your belief." Still others might think that such refutation is unloving when, in fact, it is always loving to speak the truth of God's Word. (b) As we have read throughout the Pastoral Epistles, false doctrine is dangerous. It can destroy faith and cause many to lose the gift of their salvation. Shouldn't a word of warning be spoken concerning such danger? Just as we expect to be warned of dangerous approaching storms that threaten our lives and property, should we not also expect to be warned of spiritual dangers with eternal consequences?

Day 5 • Titus 1:10–16

18. (a) The most important teaching of the Christian faith is the teaching of justification by grace, for Christ's sake, through faith. That is, we are saved not by any good works that we may do, but only because of God's love and His forgiveness in Christ, which we received through faith—trusting in Christ. (b) In Colossians chapter 2, Paul connects circumcision with the Sacrament of Holy Baptism.

19. The teachings of the circumcision group directly contradicted the teaching of justification by grace, for Christ's sake, through faith. No human works, not even circumcision, could be allowed to corrupt or water down this central teaching of the Christian faith. There could be no ambiguity on this matter.

20. (a and b) Answers will vary.

Faithful Teaching Produces Faithful Living

Titus 2–3

Preparing for the Session

Central Focus

In Titus chapter 2, Paul teaches Titus how he must preach to Christians, applying to various positions and stations in life certain exhortations and responsibilities that pertain to each. These Christians must hear the Law, gently preached to them, so that they will know what it means to live in accord with sound doctrine. This preaching of the Word will lead them to the forgiving Word of the Gospel, through which "the grace of God has appeared, bringing salvation for all people" (2:11). This grace first came to them in God's gift of Baptism, as Paul explains in chapter 3.

Objectives

That the participant, as a child of God and with the Holy Spirit's help, will be led deeper into the divinely given realizations that

1. godly and pious living results naturally from sound teaching;
2. such godliness and piety comes from God and His grace, made possible in us through the Holy Spirit, who was given in Baptism;
3. forbearance and patience toward our neighbor's temptations and sins become easier when we remember our own former foolishness and acts of impiety.

For the Small-Group Leader

Small-Group Discussion Helps

Day 1 • Titus 2:1–10

1. (a) Titus was an uncircumcised Gentile (Greek). Paul regarded him as a "true child" in the faith. He was apparently a very capable churchman, as he had served in a variety of places, including Corinth and Dalmatia. (b) At the time of this Epistle, Titus was serving on the island of Crete. The Cretans enjoyed a rather unfavorable reputation as "liars, evil beasts, lazy gluttons" (1:12).

2. Although an exact match is not possible for each quality, a variety of contrasts can be seen.

In contrast to the Cretan propensity for lying, Titus is to teach the older men to be "dignified."

In contrast to the brutish behavior of the Cretans, Titus is to teach the older men to be "sober-minded" and "sound" in faith and in love.

Rather than living as "lazy gluttons," the Cretans should exercise self-control over their gluttonous appetites and be "sound . . . in steadfastness."

3. There may be a variety of answers to this question. As a general rule, however, drunkenness tends to squelch the very qualities Paul enumerates in verse 2. Too much wine causes men to be rash instead of temperate, to act and speak in ways that cause them to lose the respect of others and to abandon all self-control. In fact, drunkenness allows the self to be easily influenced and controlled by other people, as well as by the old sinful nature.

4. (a) Rather than segregating off the younger women, Paul proposes an intergenerational approach by which the younger women would be taught and trained by the older women. Specifically, the older women could teach the younger women to love their husbands and children, to be self-controlled, and to be subject to their husbands. (b) Answers will vary.

5. The relationship between a husband and his wife should be like the relationship between *Christ* and His *church*.

6. As God's people live holy and upright lives, "they may adorn the doctrine of God our Savior." Godly living serves to enhance the beauty of godly teaching.

Day 2 • Titus 2:11–15

7. (a) The grace of God teaches us to say no to all that is ungodly and sinful. In other words, it is the Gospel (God's love for us in Christ) that generates good works and holy living. The Law cannot do this. It can only make us conscious of God's demands and our inability to meet them. (b) The notorious reputation of the Cretans might have prompted Paul to stress this particular point. After all, the Cretans were best known for their propensity to say yes to all manner of ungodliness and worldly passions. (c) This question is for personal reflec-

tion only and should simply be skipped in the small-group discussion.

8. Answers will vary. The grace of God is not without effect in those who believe. It teaches us to say no and to turn away from ungodliness and worldly passions. God's grace is sufficient to wipe away every sin, but that grace should never be construed as permission to continue on sinning. The excuses we may conjure up to justify our sinful actions will never be acceptable to God. The only remedy for human sin comes from Jesus Christ. He gave Himself on the cross for us. He redeemed us from all wickedness with His holy, precious blood and His innocent suffering and death. He alone can perfectly purify us from every sin and make us eager to do what is good. The Romans 6:1–14 text points out what our Baptism into Christ means for our daily living—that through daily contrition and repentance we may drown our old sinful flesh and free the "new person" in Christ to live before Him in righteousness.

9. When Paul writes, "The grace of God has appeared, bringing salvation for all people," the appearance he references is the appearance of Jesus in human flesh and blood. The "blessed hope" (v. 13) we wait for is His coming again.

10. Answers will vary.

Day 3 • Titus 3:1–2

11. (a) Answers will vary, but being "submissive to" someone clearly infers that honor, obedience, and respect should be shown to that person. (b) This list could include representatives from every level and branch of the government. It would include teachers at school and supervisors at work. It would include parents and grandparents, pastors, and other church leaders.

12. (a) A Christian can clearly disagree with policy decisions and express dissent over such matters without sinning. However, when disagreement over policy devolves to the level of personal attack, then God's commandment to honor such officials has been broken. Christians must also be careful to speak truthfully and accurately about the record of public officials. (b) When commanded to do something contrary to the Word of God, the Christian will always "obey God rather than men" (Acts 5:29).

13. The Christian citizen should not only be obedient but should also "be ready for every good work" (v. 1).

14. Our true comfort in this changing world comes from the fact that "our citizenship is in heaven" (Philippians 3:20). From there our Savior will come and transform our lowly bodies to be like His glorious body.

Day 4 • Titus 3:3–8

15. As Paul expresses the Gospel in these verses, he ascribes to our Savior the following qualities: kindness and love (v. 4), mercy (v. 5), and grace (v. 7).

16. He saved us . . . because of His mercy. He did not save us because of the righteous things (works) we have done.

17. The "washing" that God has given us is Holy Baptism.

18. (a) In 1 Corinthians 2:14, Paul shows the utter helplessness of each person without the Spirit. We can neither accept nor understand the things that come from the Spirit of God. We are, in effect, blind and deaf to the things of God. (b) In Ephesians 2:1, Paul describes unbelievers as "dead." Just as a dead body cannot bring itself back to life, no one without the Holy Spirit can believe in Jesus Christ or come to Him. (c) In Romans 8:7, we learn that the sinful mind is not even impartial or neutral toward God; it is hostile to God. It is unable to submit to God's Law. We would truly be lost forever apart from the washing of rebirth and renewal by the Holy Spirit.

Day 5 • Titus 3:9–15

19. (a) Paul commands that doctrinally divisive people be warned twice. If the person fails to heed those warnings, "have nothing more to do with him." (b) At least two reasons for this drastic action can be distilled from 1 Corinthians 5. There Paul commands that an immoral member of the Corinthian congregation be expelled "for the destruction of the flesh, so that his spirit may be saved in the day of the Lord" (v. 5). In other words, expelling the unrepentant sinner serves as a final attempt to bring about repentance. Second, Paul warns of how "a little leaven leavens the whole lump" (v. 6). Just as a tiny amount of yeast is able to affect an entire batch of dough, so the public sins and heresy of one man, if left unaddressed, could negatively affect the entire congregation. Thus, action must be taken against such divisive people so that others are not led astray.

20. Encourage the participants to think of as many ways to support mission as possible. Cite examples from your own congregation. Financial gifts, prayers, personal correspondence with missionaries, mite boxes, and the forming of congregational mission societies are just scratching the surface as ways to support world missions.

21. We make this request of our heavenly Father every time we pray "Thy kingdom come."

Love for Neighbor Arises from Faith

Philemon

Preparing for the Session

Central Focus

Paul repeats the phrase *in Christ* throughout this short Letter, revealing that our treatment of our neighbor is rooted in nothing other than the Gospel. Paul's request that Philemon welcome back the escaped slave Onesimus provides us with the opportunity to contemplate our own treatment of our neighbor within the context of God's grace shown to us *in Christ.*

Objectives

That the participant, as a child of God and with the Holy Spirit's help, will be led deeper into the divinely given realizations that

1. even though the Letter to Philemon does not expressly discuss Christian teaching, the Gospel of Christ forms the background for the things that are written here;
2. the Gospel is not merely for our Sunday morning worship, but it permeates every aspect of our life in this world;
3. our treatment of our neighbor is rooted in the gracious treatment Christ has given us through His death and resurrection.

For the Small-Group Leader

Small-Group Discussion Helps

Day 1 • Philemon 1–3

1. (a) Paul typically identifies himself as an "apostle" at the beginning of each of his Epistles. That self-designation is missing in his Letter to Philemon. (b) Although we can only speculate the reason for this omission, it could stem from the purpose of this Letter. He was asking no small thing from Philemon—namely, that he would receive back his runaway slave, Onesimus, as a brother in Christ. Paul further hints that *he* would benefit greatly if Onesimus could be permitted to return to him and continue his personal service to Paul. In making such a bold request, Paul perhaps thought it wise not to assert his apostolic authority but to take a more humble, brotherly approach. Similarly, Paul wanted any favors from Philemon to be "not by compulsion but of your own free will," a further reason to eschew his apostolic title.

2. In Colossians chapter 4, Paul describes Onesimus as "our faithful and beloved brother." By designating Onesimus as "one of you" to the Colossians, it seems likely that Colosse was Onesimus's home town. He, together with Tychicus, had been sent by Paul to relay news about Paul's ministry.

3. (a) Philemon's home also served as a meeting place for the church. (b) As an owner of slaves and possessing a bigger than average home, it seems likely that Philemon was a wealthy man.

4. (a) God's grace is personified and expressed most clearly in Jesus Christ. In Ephesians 1:6, Paul writes of the "glorious grace" of God, "with which he has blessed us in the Beloved." (b) Through faith in Jesus Christ we now enjoy a twofold peace—peace with God (Rom. 5:1), and peace with our fellow human beings. Ephesians 2:14–18 specifically addresses the "person-to-person" peace Christ achieved between Jews and Gentiles "by abolishing the law of commandments and ordinances."

5. It would be only a partial victory if Philemon forgave Onesimus and welcomed him back as a brother in Christ while the members of Philemon's family and the congregation that met in his home continued to harbor bitter feelings of anger and resentment against the former fugitive. Paul's persuasive words to Philemon might, at some point, need to be shared with members of his family and church.

Day 2 • Philemon 4–7

6. (a) Just as Philemon was remembered by Paul in his prayers, Paul had also been remembered by Philemon in his prayers. Specifically, Philemon had prayerfully desired that Paul would be able to visit him in Colosse.

(b) Paul had heard about Philemon's love of "all the saints" (v. 5). He now hoped that Philemon would receive Onesimus back, guided and prompted by that same remarkable love. (c) Paul's own heart would be "refreshed" to see Onesimus received and welcomed by Philemon as a dear brother.

7. It is especially as Christians gather for the Divine Service that their fellowship with other believers is actively expressed. By actively hearing and studying the doctrine of the apostles, by praying for the needs of the whole world, and by joining together in the breaking of bread (The Lord's Supper) Christians today can be "active in sharing" (NIV) their faith.

8. Answers will vary.

9. It probably would have reminded Philemon that he and Paul shared a Father in heaven—and also shared a Brother, who gave Himself as a sacrifice for their sins. *Brother* is also a warm and disarming word—a word that would have appealed to Philemon's very heart.

Day 3 • Philemon 8–14

10. (a) Had Paul taken the "vinegar" approach, he would have simply ordered Philemon to do what he wanted done. Such an order would have been grounded in Paul's apostolic authority. Philemon, for his part, would have been forced to follow the order of his apostolic superior. (b) The "honey" approach taken by Paul was an appeal and not an order. It was made on the basis of love and not on the basis of Paul's status and authority as an apostle.

11. Paul wanted to establish the basis for his request concerning Onesimus before mentioning the runaway slave by name. Only after reminding Philemon of their shared faith and brotherly relationship would Paul proceed to the heart of the matter. By making no initial mention of Onesimus, Paul made it easier for Philemon to "hear" his request and muted any harsh feelings that the name of Onesimus might have otherwise elicited.

12. (a) Timothy and Titus were both regarded by Paul as sons. (b) Answers will vary. By calling Onesimus his "child," Paul was tactfully showing Philemon the love and appreciation that he had for Onesimus. Philemon probably needed to hear Onesimus described in this way since he likely hadn't felt much love or appreciation for Onesimus since he ran away.

13. (a) Answers will (obviously) vary! (b) Some appropriate names for those who believe in Christ include "loved," "holy," "splendor," and "without blemish" (Ephesians 5:25–27); "pure" and "blameless" (Philippians 1:10); "chosen," "beloved" (Colossians 3:12). Other possible names would be "saint," "blessed," or "righteous."

14. Good works in God's sight are those that are done willingly and spontaneously, not under compulsion. Good works are done freely and from the heart, in response to God's love in Christ.

Day 4 • Philemon 15–25

15. (a) In Romans 8:28, we have the amazing promise that "for those who love God all things work together for good, for those who are called according to His purpose." (b) When Onesimus ran away from Philemon, he thought he was gaining his freedom. But then he met St. Paul, who gave him true freedom by leading him to faith in Jesus Christ. Now, through the inspired words of St. Paul's Epistle to Philemon, there could be forgiveness and reconciliation between Philemon and Onesimus. Now, instead of owning a mere slave, Philemon received back a brother in Christ, eager to do what is right and good. (c) Answers will vary.

16. Just as Onesimus had "done wrong" to Philemon by running away, we have wronged our heavenly Father in thought, word, and deed. Just as Paul assumed the debt Philemon had incurred by fleeing, the debt of our sin was "charged" to Jesus. He "paid back" all we owe. Paul wrote concerning Onesimus, "Receive him as you would receive me." With faith in Jesus Christ and covered with His righteousness, we will one day be welcomed into the Father's presence as beloved sons and daughters.

Day 5 • Colossians 3:22–4:1

17. The works of service we perform according to our various life callings are ultimately done for the Lord. He is the one we are serving as we serve our families and neighbors. God delights in our works of service, even those that we might consider unimportant and inconsequential.

18. They should all be mindful that they themselves have a Master in heaven. Whatever authority they may now possess is a gift from the Master in heaven. It should be exercised and expressed accordingly.

19. Answers will vary.

PGIL2024USA